Praise for *Stop Struggling with Your Child*

"An absolute must for parents, teachers and counselors who want immediate solutions to everyday problems. A fun, fast read."
—Doris Wild Helmering, columnist, *St. Louis Post-Dispatch*

"*Stop Struggling with Your Child* has been very helpful in keeping me focused as a parent. It is refreshingly written, and a good reference piece for those days when you need some straight answers. It works!"
—Donna Klein, Director of Work and Family Life, Marriott Corporation

"Hollywood should take a few pages from Evonne and Karen, who clearly know how to produce a sequel as good or better than the original. *Stop Struggling with Your Child* is an impressive follow-up to *Stop Struggling with Your Teen.*"
—George Marcelle, former Public Information Director, National Council on Alcoholism and Drug Dependence

"This is the best approach to parenting I've read. It pinpoints the skills parents need to help their children become responsible decision-makers, cooperative team players and confident self-motivators."
—Joyce Lain Kennedy, columnist, Los Angeles Times Syndicate

"The skills in this easy-to-read, example-filled book are wonderfully teachable and apply to all children. I especially liked that it can be used by families with children who have special health care needs."
—Kay Bartholomew, community health educator, Houston, Texas

Stop Struggling with Your Child

Stop Struggling with Your Child

EVONNE WEINHAUS and
KAREN FRIEDMAN

Illustrations by Lillian Habinowski

HarperPerennial
A Division of HarperCollins*Publishers*

Workshops and Lectures

If you are interested in learning about our Stop Struggling with Your Child presentations or workshops, or would like to be on our mailing list, please contact us at:

Stop Struggling
P.O. Box 9138
St. Louis, MO 63117

FIRST EDITION

Designed by Helene Berinsky

Library of Congress Cataloging-in-Publication Data

Weinhaus, Evonne.
    Stop struggling with your child / Evonne Weinhaus and Karen
Friedman.—1st ed.
        p.   cm.
    ISBN 0-06-055193-3
    ISBN 0-06-096481-2 (pbk.)
    1. Child rearing—United States.   2. Child psychology—United
States.   3. Self-respect in children.   I. Friedman, Karen, 1950–.
II. Title.
HQ769.W427   1991   89-46493
649′.1—dc20

91 92 93 94 95 CC/MPC 10 9 8 7 6 5 4 3 2 1
   92 93 94 95 CC/MPC 10 9 8 7 6 5   (pbk.)

We'd like to dedicate this book to all the parents who came to us after we wrote Stop Struggling with Your Teen *saying, "What about our younger kids?" This book is for you.*

We would also like to thank those who broke ground in the field of parent education: Rudolf Dreikurs, Thomas Gordon, and Robert and Jean Bayard. Our book is based on many of their ideas.

Contents

Acknowledgments

First and foremost we want to say a big thank-you to our families for putting up with us throughout the writing of this book. Each of you has contributed your own unique brand of patience and support. We'd also like to thank Bea for her faithful pampering and Janet Goldstein, our editor, who was right more often than we'd like to admit. Finally, we want to acknowledge all the parents we've worked with over the years for their enthusiasm, willingness to share, and compassion.

Quick Tips at Your Fingertips

I: START WITH STRUCTURE

Don't Use Your Mouth, Use Your Routine

Instead of providing order all day long with your words, set up clear, daily structure beforehand. Then cut down on directing as you learn to choose your words wisely and sparingly.

If You Can't Change the Child, Change the Environment

Make concrete changes in the physical setup of the household so the environment, not you, dictates the rules, while your child enjoys some independence.

Follow Up with Follow-Through

Start with routines and rules that rely on *your* follow-through, not your child's. Let the consequences be your kid's reminder and your salvation.

Stay Grounded with Ground Rules

Stick to your nonnegotiable rules, and keep your credibility. You can stay grounded and keep your kids from breaking you down with their masterful use of logic and reason.

Go for Negotiation

Create rules *with* your children, not just for them. They will be more likely to cooperate, and rules can be seen as a positive tool to create order rather than a weapon used to clobber your kids.

II: BUILD RESPONSIBILITY

Turn Tasks into Tidbits

Ensure a feeling of success by cutting independent tasks into manageable, bite-size pieces. You can start with the young child, small decisions, and small responsibilities. Rather than focus on important, overwhelming issues, use the seemingly insignificant activities that fill every child's day.

Keep Your Kid in the Director's Chair

Try to avoid taking over your kids' responsibilities no matter how hard they try to get you involved. Balance your decision to hand responsibility back with a supportive, caring attitude.

Treat 'Em as a Team

Sibling relationships are a great place to teach your kids to be cooperative team players. So during sibling fights, instead of dividing your kids or showing favoritism by taking sides, unite your kids and encourage *them* to problem-solve and learn important relationship skills.

III: SHORT-CIRCUIT POWER STRUGGLES

Diffuse, Don't Ignite, Conflict

Sidestep unnecessary struggles with silence or with brief or humorous responses. When you avoid your own defensive maneuvers, your children will have no need for theirs.

Use Motion, Not Emotion

When your anger is at its peak, instead of highlighting emotions with words, make your point with action. You can walk with your legs, point with your finger, or even use pantomime as you move away from the power struggle.

Make a Correction with a Connection

Make a connection between the child's misdeed and the resulting discipline. Whenever possible, let him experience the consequences of his behavior.

Stick with Consequences

Stay consistent and teach with consequences, even when it seems easier and quicker not to.

IV: MAXIMIZE SELF-ESTEEM

Make the Most of Ho-Hum Moments

The key to being encouraging even in the hardest of times is to realize the importance of the simple, everyday happenings that are all too often ignored.

Tune In to Your Kids so They Don't Tune Out

Instead of always working so hard at making your children

understand what *you* say, work hard at understanding and acknowledging what *they* say.

Make the Evidence Evident

Rather than focus on your child's potential, focus on your child's current, irrefutable accomplishments by describing what you see and remembering his past, already mastered accomplishments.

See the Small Successes along the Way

While it's okay to praise good results, you can multiply your self-esteem builders by highlighting the many small steps that occur as your child tackles each task.

Getting Started

Wouldn't it be nice to open this book and finally find that magical, foolproof, money-back-guaranteed formula for raising that perfectly adjusted child in that perfectly harmonious household. While we certainly could never claim to have discovered that well-kept secret, we'd like to offer you some hope and some help in the form of this parenting handbook. It's a culmination of our work with our clients, our teaching of parenting groups and, of course, our own adventures through parenthood.

We have started this book with typical, small problems. As we move along, we build our way up to more difficult problems as you build your way up to more complex parenting skills. Those of you who are brushing up on your parenting skills can start from the beginning and move along at a leisurely pace with the structure of the book as you integrate some new skills with your own approach. If you are feeling desperate and you want to tackle a particular problem area immediately, feel free to locate the appropriate chapter and begin there. You can always backtrack at a later date. The important point is that you use this book as a tool to meet your own needs. If you start small and stick with the changes you make, you will notice a difference in your household in no time at all.

We have divided the book into four sections that represent the areas we believe to be the building blocks for any effective, loving parenting approach:

- Start with structure: Replace chaos with rules and routines.
- Build responsibility: Foster self-reliance and independence.
- Short-circuit power   Move from conflict to
  struggles: cooperation.
- Build self-esteem: Encourage confident, happy children.

Each of these sections is broken down further into short, easy-to-remember quick tips that are filled with ways to reduce conflict and build self-esteem while respecting a child's natural style and abilities.

When you begin to read our examples, you will notice that we have not mentioned the ages of the children. Most of the behavior and all of the skills discussed are appropriate for all school-age children. So when you are reading a section and feel that the child in the example must be a clone of your six-year-old son, don't be surprised if another parent insists the story is about his eleven-year-old daughter, for that's exactly what happened to us. Both of us fervently believed that one of our examples was taken from an experience with our own sons. The boys, Seth and Eddie, happen to be eight years apart. After arguing about which child it really was, we decided to capitalize on this discovery and let you share the experience of identifying your own child in the many examples throughout the book. In fact, you may even find a parent who sounds remarkably like you. So enjoy the familiarity, sit back, and get ready to stop struggling with your child.

Start with Structure

It is amazing how much we know about parenting before we have children, and how little we know once we become parents ourselves. Before we have children we know just how to avoid making the mistakes our parents made; we know just how to teach important values to our children; and we know exactly how to handle those temper tantrums that we see other parents mismanage as they try to navigate the grocery store with their screaming children.

And then we have our own. What happens to all that confidence and knowledge? If we're lucky, we can hold on to it briefly as we marvel at that adorable baby who can do no wrong. But in no time at all that newborn who melted us with a simple toothless smile, and who was applauded for burping immediately after his feeding, is challenging us in ways we never imagined and bringing commotion into our once orderly lives.

This is especially true when parents are overwhelmed as they find themselves moving from one crisis to the next. They feel like their days are filled with chaos and commotion and they don't know where to start to get some cooperation and peace. We'd like to suggest that a good place to begin making changes is with the small, simple rules and routines that make up the structure of the household.

Structure is important for two reasons: It provides an atmosphere of safety, security, and predictability for any child; and it is the easiest way to reduce a lot of unnecessary frustration that can creep into the day and result in pouts, tears, and struggles.

Even the most flexible parents will learn soon enough that when they begin by making small, simple changes in their rules and routines, they see immediate results as chaos diminishes. While many parents ultimately make heroic efforts to create rules and routines, we'd like to stress the following point: It's not just important *that* parents provide some structure, it's important *how* they provide that structure. All too often, without meaning to, they go about it in ways that produce more friction than peace, more dependence than independence. Their attempts to provide predictability lead to conflict.

In the pages that follow you will learn how to avoid that friction as you learn five simple ways to ease rules and routines into your family life:

- Don't use your mouth, use your routine.
- If you can't change the child, change the environment.
- Follow up with follow-through.
- Stay grounded with ground rules.
- Go for negotiation.

Believe it or not, your household can operate with a smoother, more harmonious rhythm.

Quick Tip

Don't Use Your Mouth, Use Your Routine

Instead of providing order all day long with your words, set up clear, daily structure beforehand. Then cut down on directing as you learn to choose your words wisely and sparingly.

The first and most common mistake many parents make when they try to promote structure is to rely way too much on talking and directing. Out of frustration, parents say things like

"You know you can't eat that junk before dinner."

"Haven't you put your pajamas on yet?"

"Hurry up. You're going to miss the school bus again!"

"You better have your homework done before you put on that TV!"

While these remarks are usually well-intentioned efforts to enforce rules and routines, they end up creating unnecessary tension between parents and kids. When said with any frequency, these verbal messages often leave children feeling blamed or criticized. Parents need to learn to stop depending on a seemingly endless flow of directions to create routines.

Instead of trying to establish order all day long with words, you can set up structure beforehand, then begin to cut down on your directing as you choose your words wisely and sparingly. The simple change of reducing your directing can make all the difference in the world.

To give you an idea of what we mean, let's take a look at the saga of Mrs. L, a frustrated mother who started her mornings in a frenzy until she learned a new way of talking to her son.

Mrs. L is the mother of a boy we shall affectionately call Johnny-Come-Lately, a name he worked hard to earn. Like most parents, Mrs. L had set up a reasonable, natural morning routine for her child: get up, get dressed, have breakfast, and head off to school with a smile and a warm hug. To her credit, she started off perfectly. She stated the routine clearly to Johnny. In fact, she stated it more times than she cared to remember. Somehow it was not working like it did on those family television shows of the 1950s, when everyone began the morning sitting around the kitchen table eating hot cereal and making pleasant conversation. Instead, her mornings were spent constantly issuing directions, which she believed should help move her son through a nice, normal morning routine.

As you read about just one of her many miserable mornings with Johnny, you will surely understand Mrs. L's flight into madness. As she so aptly put it, she was transformed from a helpful, sweet mom into the "nag queen." Here's how a typical morning went.

Mrs. L gently woke Johnny with her usual morning hug as she told him it was time to get up. But minutes passed, and Johnny stayed blissfully asleep.

"Johnny, time to get up. You'll be late," Mrs. L called out.

As usual, Mrs. L found herself making quite a few trips back into Johnny's room, and her gentle tone became a memory.

"Come on. Get up and get going! You better leave enough time to find that library book," she said. When twenty minutes had passed, and her son was still in bed with few signs of life, she felt she was ready to burst. This kid was getting up or else.

"Johnny, I've told you at least ten times to get up. How many times do I have to say the same thing?"

He crawled slowly out of bed, feeling his way to the bathroom.

"Don't forget to brush your teeth and comb your hair. You have to move faster than that if you expect to eat breakfast."

Time continued to march on, while Johnny didn't. The school bus was nearly due, and Johnny still had not eaten, or finished dressing. Mrs. L was at her wit's end, searching for any way possible to get him going. She resorted to empty threats, issued as she served breakfast to her half-dressed son. "If you're not ready in five minutes, no television after school for three days." She followed this with the usual promise she made but

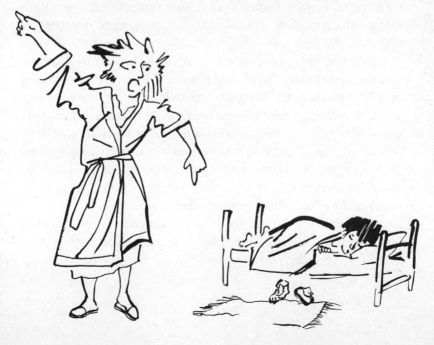

never quite kept: "I will just make you go to bed earlier, and get up earlier in the morning."

Although Mrs. L was trying to establish a workable routine, she and Johnny had become immersed in a routine of chaos, a routine that kept Mom chronically directing and Johnny chronically depending on directions.

Mrs. L knew she had to do something different, but she was at a loss. When she told us her plight, it was clear to us that she had to start by changing *her own behavior* rather than expecting Johnny to change his. She had to find a way to replace her talking and take herself out of the role of commander in chief. Rather than rely on commands and threats to change Johnny, she needed to talk less and at the same time say more. She needed to start with this quick tip: Don't use your mouth, use your routine.

The first and most obvious step Mrs. L could take to reduce her directing was to get an alarm clock for Johnny—one with a nice loud buzzer. At first Mrs. L was not sold on the notion that an alarm clock was the answer, but we assured her that this was only the first step.

Her next task was going to be a lot more challenging. She was going to change what and how much she said to Johnny, and, though she thoroughly believed Johnny would never make it without those chronic reminders, she was desperate enough to give our suggestions a try. After her part was well-rehearsed, Mrs. L strolled into Johnny's room at wake-up time and presented the alarm clock. She, of course, found him in his usual laid-out position, and she fought the urge to lecture. Instead she made these simple statements:

"I bought you a new alarm clock, and it is set to go off in five minutes. This will be a great way for you to get up. And just think, you won't have to listen to me hound you all morning."

Then she bit her tongue and retreated to her room. Mrs. L was a realist. While she secretly hoped the alarm would be enough to get Johnny up, she was more confident that Johnny would not jump out of bed and cheerfully embrace the day. She was prepared with her next set of statements as Johnny drifted back to slumberland.

As time passed and her stomach began to tighten, she knocked on the door and said:

"It's 7:45. The school bus will be here in thirty minutes."

"I'm just finishing dressing. I'll meet you in the kitchen for breakfast."

Then she forced herself into the kitchen and got busy getting breakfast on the table. Keeping busy was a good way for her to avoid falling back into her familiar, ineffective morning madness.

Before we continue, let's take a closer look at the new communication skills Mrs. L was using:

✳ *Spotlight Your Own Action*

"I bought you a new alarm clock, and it is set to go off in five minutes."

This skill does just what it says; it spotlights the parent's action—not the child's. It tells the child what the parent will be doing differently. "I" is the subject of the sentence, not "you." This is the kind of statement you can use to replace "You better . . ." or "You should . . ." or "Haven't you . . ." and all the other ways parents point their fingers at their children.

✳ *Point Out the Benefit*

> *"This will be a great way for you to get up. And just think, you won't have to listen to me hound you all morning."*

The difference between this statement and "I'm tired of coming in here ten times every morning; you'll just have to use an alarm clock" is rather obvious. Instead of using a routine as a threat, show your child that the change will make life easier. It is very important that your child realize the new routine is not a punishment but an improved way to deal with an old problem.

✳ *State the Facts without Blame*

> *"It's 7:45. The school bus will be here in thirty minutes."*

This skill sticks with the facts—nothing but the facts. By uttering *one* brief reminder, you can avoid blaming, criticizing comments like "Are you still dawdling? You're going to be late as usual." You can make your point without the judgmental remarks that create resentment and rebellion. You'll know you've got this skill right when the *fact,* not your child, is the subject of the sentence.

✳ *Set a House Routine*

> *"I'm just finishing dressing. I'll meet you in the kitchen for breakfast."*

It hardly needs saying that kids pick up a lot more cues from what we do than from what we say. Consequently, when we can it's best to introduce routine as something that applies to all members of the house. In this case, getting dressed *before* breakfast is a routine *everyone* can follow. By creating a house routine, we avoid pointing our finger at a culprit, and we also show that the routine is important enough for everyone to follow.

As we mentioned, Mrs. L rehearsed her lines before putting them to use. When just beginning to use these skills, it's often helpful to figure out what you're going to say before you say it. This keeps you from resorting to that all too familiar tendency to nag or preach. Like Mrs. L, every parent has a cutoff point—a point where talking turns into screaming and lecturing. To avoid reaching that point, you need to limit yourself to three or four sentences. While this may seem unnatural or contrived, it will help keep tempers from flaring. Mrs. L did just that. She kept herself to the four skills that set up structure without nagging. And she did this despite her desire to apply some verbal pressure to move Johnny along.

Mrs. L reported that, as the days passed, Johnny was beginning to realize that she was not going to jump in and start her directing routine. And Mrs. L came to realize that Johnny was quite capable of moving himself through a natural morning routine without her constant prodding. Of course, things did not go perfectly in the L household. For the first few weeks, Johnny seemed like he'd never get it together. One morning his hair was unbrushed. His coat and lunch box were under one arm, as he tried to balance the shoe and sock he hadn't quite managed to get on yet in his other hand. Quite to Johnny's surprise, Mrs. L gently "escorted" him out the front door despite the fact that he seemed to be carrying more clothes than he was wearing.

On the whole, though, life was different in the L household. Mrs. L had set up a routine that did not depend on chronic directing. She knew her lines and moves, and, most important, she consistently followed them. When the routine didn't go exactly as planned, Mom was not in a frenzy (even when Johnny was), and that was a welcome switch.

For both Johnny and Mrs. L, the immediate result of less chaos and less fighting was welcome. But there was another result, equally important though not quite as obvious. The change at home created changes in other areas of Johnny's life. It should not surprise anyone that Johnny's reliance on chronic adult directing and prodding occurred elsewhere too. He had become used to expecting Mom and other adults, such as teachers, to move him along, even when he was quite capable of moving under his own steam. The change in the morning routine was an excellent step toward teaching Johnny the importance of moving himself along not just at home but across the board. While Mrs. L's short-range goal of changing her language was to diminish the tension and floundering in their morning routine, the more important long-range goal of helping Johnny move himself was also accomplished, and this is a lesson he will be able to carry with him into all areas of his life.

As you begin to use your words wisely and sparingly in your own home, you may want to follow Mrs. L's lead and start with your morning routine. Mornings are often a good place to begin strengthening routines for two reasons. First, morning often sets the tone for the rest of the day. While a good morning may not ensure a good day, a bad morning can result in a bad day. Second, morning is not just a routine of the household, it's a natural routine of the day. Starting with natural routines such as morning, bedtime, or after-school snack gives you some additional help as you try to diminish your talking, help that comes from following the regular flow of the day. So, take advantage of the natural order of every day when you begin to rely less on your mouth and more on your routine.

As you start to limit your words, you will notice that everyone will benefit:

- Your child pays attention when you do talk because there is less overall nagging.
- Your child doesn't feel punished, harassed, or victimized.
- Your child feels more independent.
- You feel less frazzled and angry.

POINTS TO REMEMBER

1. Remember that structure gives your family the security and predictability that diminish chaos.

2. Choose your words wisely and sparingly, and let the routines of the day direct your child.

3. Don't clobber your child with rules and routines. Introduce them as helpful problem-solving strategies.

4. Role model your routine when possible.

5. Use natural routines of the day to help set up household routines.

6. Remember that small changes in daily routines can have far-reaching benefits in all areas of your child's life.

7. Use the following communication skills to keep your directing to a minimum:

> * *Spotlight your own action.*
>
> * *Point out the benefit.*
>
> * *State the facts without blame.*
>
> * *Set a house routine.*

If You Can't Change the Child, Change the Environment

Make concrete changes in the physical setup of the household so the environment, not you, dictates the rules, while your child enjoys some independence.

Now many of you may be just about ready to strangle us as we calmly suggest that when you consistently choose your words wisely and sparingly your kid will more readily follow household rules and routines. You may be thinking, "Maybe that will be enough for some kids, but not mine."

We fully believe that changes can be achieved by altering the way you talk to your kid when you implement routines. But we are also aware that there will be some circumstances in which changing routines and language needs to be accompanied by changes in the environment. That's just what one mother, Mrs. H, needed to learn as she struggled with the dilemma of how to keep her kids away from junk food without banning it from the house entirely.

One afternoon while she was stirring a pot with one hand and grabbing the chips from her kids, Lauren and Mike, with the other, Mrs. H realized she had to deal once and for all with the afternoon invasion of the pantry. She had already tried the reasonable approach, explaining the drawbacks of too much

15

junk food. And she had tried the setting-the-rule approach, establishing a policy of no sweets after 4:30. Essentially, her children let Mom's words go in one ear and out the other as they vied for the last few potato chip crumbs. Their response to her rule setting was to test it and test it and test it as they kept her busy with their attempts to persuade her:

"Can't I have another cookie just this once?"

"It's no fair. Lauren got a Popsicle and I didn't!"

Mrs. H barely had enough time to catch her breath as she tried to field these seemingly endless pleas.

On the verge of a major blowup with her kids, Mrs. H needed additional help that would move her out of her role as food police officer. When she came to our parenting group for advice, it was already clear to her that she couldn't change her kids. So we suggested that she try to find a simple way to change the environment instead. Once she had this new idea to get her going, she put her creativity to work. This is how Mrs. H resolved her dilemma. First, she moved all the junk food out of the kids' reach. Then she emptied two small drawers in the kitchen and put Lauren's name on one and Mike's on the other. Finally, she used some structuring skills to implement the new routine.

As soon as the kids got home from school, she explained,

"I have made each of you a snack drawer, and I will fill them with fruit, vegetables, raisins, and other nutritious food. [spotlight your own action]

"If you're hungry before dinner, you can help yourself to a snack without asking." [point out the benefit]

Did Mrs. H's kids immediately stop begging for sweets? Of course not, at least not right away. They continued to test Mom to see if the snack drawer was a passing fancy or a permanent change. But with the benefit of simple communication skills and her change in the environment, Mrs. H was able to stick to her guns. Over time she helped the process along even more by getting her children involved in choosing some of the snacks for their drawers.

Mrs. H was able to change the environment in an encouraging, matter-of-fact way. She initiated the change, provided the structure, and was concrete and specific. Her kids knew the limits exactly and could take responsibility for getting their own snacks. Ultimately, she gave them some independence, and she gave herself peace of mind, knowing her kids wouldn't be inhaling junk food all afternoon.

In the same way that Mrs. H changed the environment and cut down on her struggles over snacks, Mrs. E resolved her struggles with her daughter, Alyson, over clothes. Like Johnny-Come-Lately's mother, Mrs. E complained about her morning routine. She did not have a problem getting her daughter up, but she did have a problem avoiding time-consuming battles over what clothes to wear. Mom wanted to wear Mom's clothes, and Alyson, all of a sudden, wanted to wear Mom's clothes too. Somehow, Alyson began to take an unprecedented interest in Mom's T-shirts, sweaters, socks, and so forth. On an all too regular basis, she would begin the morning plowing through her mother's dresser looking for that certain shirt. Mrs. E was not opposed to sharing a few things, but the clashes began to grow as she found herself constantly monitoring Alyson's expanding interest in her clothes.

Here's how things would go:

ALYSON: Can I wear your blue shirt to school today?

MRS. E: Alyson, I was not planning to "share" my shirt with you. I haven't worn it myself yet.

ALYSON: You weren't going to wear it today, so I want to.

MRS. E: No, you're not. I don't mind you wearing some of my stuff, but you can't just take whatever you want.

ALYSON: I promise I won't get it dirty. I really like that color on me.

MRS. E: No, not today.

There are a couple of ways Mrs. E could have handled the situation. She could have lectured and explained, but, as we've seen, this is rarely effective. She could have realized that this

is a fairly typical developmental phase and just hung in there until the next phase. However, this philosophical approach only works for those who can handle the morning standoff with ease or don't mind starting the day with a headache. Or she could have turned the morning battle around by changing the environment. In this case, Mrs. E changed the environment by rearranging a hallway dresser drawer. She pulled out all the items from her wardrobe that she was willing to "share" and put them in the hallway drawer. Then she posted off-limits signs on her bedroom closet and dresser.

Here's what Mrs. E said to Alyson:

> *"I've put the clothes I want to share in the hallway drawer.* [spotlight your own action]
>
> *"If you want to borrow something of mine, you know where you can find it, and you don't have to ask."* [point out the benefit]

Now, instead of arguing about what to wear, Alyson's mom has the opportunity to compliment her daughter on how nice she looks. She has also turned a conflictful situation around and can still share some of her clothes.

By finally seeing the light and cooperating with the change in her environment, Alyson maintained some access to her mom's wardrobe. In our next example, Chrissy had nothing to gain, nothing, that is, except the opportunity to make her bed. And what child was ever motivated by that!

Chrissy tried every possible excuse to escape the morning routine of making her bed. But her mother, Mrs. M, wanted that bed made. She tried several approaches, including coopera-tion, as in "I'll help you make the bed"; idle ultimatums, as in

"That bed better be made before you go to school"; and bargaining, as in "I'll pay you a quarter each morning you make your bed."

Nothing worked. There was no way Chrissy would take that extra time to make her bed.

Applying the quick tip "If you can't change the child, change the environment," Mrs. M came up with the following idea:

> *"I will sew together two sheets and put your comforter in between the sheets. [spotlight your own action]*
>
> *"This way the cover can be thrown over the bed, and— presto—the bed will be made." [point out the benefit]*

Believe it or not, Chrissy liked this solution and was willing to go along with it, at least most of the time. By changing the environment, Mrs. M created a win-win situation. The bed got made, as she wished, and Chrissy avoided the conventional struggle with sheets. Most important, Chrissy learned that creative ideas can bring solutions to seemingly deadlocked situations.

The principle used in these three examples is simple: By talking less and structuring the environment more, these parents got their point across. Mrs. M was able to get the job done with a new comforter, Mrs. E with her new way of arranging clothes, and Mrs. H with the food drawers.

Instead of trying to change your child's behavior with constant directing and advising, you can make concrete changes in the physical setup of your household. The environment then dictates the necessary limits and establishes the routines—you don't. There is no doubt that the result is less fighting and more cooperation as your child learns from doing rather than being told what to do.

POINTS TO REMEMBER

1. When changing your language is not enough, add a change in the environment, and give your child visible, concrete cues to help set limits and establish routine.

2. Present your changes in the environment as a helpful way for your child to rely more on himself and less on your reminding. Changes presented as threats and punishments are rarely as effective.

3. Once you've created a change in the environment, bow out and let your child take over. If you find yourself continuing to direct, you probably need to set up a different, more effective environmental change.

4. When you set up a change in the environment, use the following communication skills:

    ❊ *Spotlight your own action.*

    ❊ *Point out the benefit.*

Follow Up with Follow-Through

Start with routine and rules that rely on your follow-through—not your child's. Let the consequences be your kid's reminder and your salvation.

Thus far we've discussed how parents can replace chaos with structure by implementing the following quick tips:

1. Don't use your mouth, use your routine.

2. If you can't change the child, change the environment.

As we've seen, once these principles are in place, the chaos decreases and the sense of structure increases. When parents follow their change in language with a change in the environment, they can almost guarantee a more cooperative outcome.

Still, there are many times when parents want to set up rules or routines that cannot be implemented with a simple change in the environment. For example,

- You want your child in bed by 8:30.
- You want all the books off the kitchen table before dinner.
- You want the special treats you buy for the kids to last the week.
- You want your children to buckle their seat belts as soon as they get in the car.

How do you implement these rules and routines without reverting to the old habit of lecturing? You can still start by spotlighting your own action, but you can reinforce the message with a little extra zing—a consequence that depends on your follow-through. Here's what we mean.

Instead of saying,

"You have to be in bed by 8:30."

"Get those books off the dining room table now. How do you expect me to put dinner out with this mess?"

"Don't eat all the cookies at once."

"You better buckle up your seat belts."

you can use the following:

✳ *Spotlight Your Own Action with a Consequence*

"I'll read you a story after teeth are brushed, pajamas are on, and before your 8:30 bedtime."

"I'll serve dinner after the table is cleared of books."

"I will buy cookies once a week, and I'll get more next week when I go grocery shopping."

"I will start the car when your seat belts are on."

These statements create a consequence that *you* carry out. For example,

- The consequence of not getting ready by 8:30 is no story.
- The consequence of not clearing the table is delayed dinner.
- The consequence of devouring all the cookies in one full sweep is no more cookies until the next shopping day.
- The consequence of not buckling seat belts is not starting the car.

The key is this: Instead of you reminding your child ad nauseam, the consequence does the reminding for you.

There will be occasions when you need to marshal all your forces to make an impact on your child. You will want to limit your words, change the environment, and spotlight your action with a consequence. Putting these strategies together can dramatically improve a child's ability and willingness to follow through. We can see how this works by looking at perhaps the most universal of problems—children neglecting to pick up after themselves. This problem constantly plagued one mother, Mrs. B, who struggled with her messy son, whom we shall call Terry the Trailblazer.

Terry was a detective's dream. As he raced through the house, he dropped his books and papers, followed closely by a jacket, hat, and glove. His shoes were usually hidden under a bed or couch. His distinctive trail had one and only one advantage. Mrs. B always knew where to find him; she just followed the path.

Unlike Terry, Mrs. B was neat, and she valued having a neat home. Her goal was to make Terry pick up his belongings and put them away. She was tired of reminding him daily, only to hear those miserable words "In a minute, Mom." But the worst part wasn't the mess, it was the fact that Terry would blame *her* when he couldn't find something.

Here's an example. One morning Mrs. B just couldn't wait to report her run-in with Terry to the parenting group. Terry was furious with her because *she* couldn't find his math homework. Mrs. B was torn. There was a part of her that did not want to help Terry because she knew the missing work was his fault, not hers. But then again, it was his homework; he had done the assignment, and she didn't want Terry to get a zero for work he had completed. In her frustration, she did what many mothers do. She screamed, "Why don't you put your papers away when you're done with them? I'm not helping you!" as she looked through his folder. As you can imagine, it was not the first time this scenario had been played out.

Mrs. B was tired. In her desperation, she was ready to let the group help her. She wanted to

1. Have an orderly house

2. Stop fighting with Terry about his stuff

3. Have Terry begin to take some responsibility for his own belongings instead of blaming others

With these three goals in mind, we were able to suggest a new routine that used both change in the environment and a consequence that would depend on Mrs. B's follow-through. Mrs. B took a very important first step when she went home and implemented her new routine. She picked the right moment to relate her new approach. She didn't scream her idea in anger while she was holding up someone's sock that had never made it to the hamper. She chose a moment when she, Dad, and the kids were sitting around the dinner table feeling full and relatively happy. We've abbreviated the reported conversation to illustrate the skills Mrs. B used:

MRS. B: From now on, when stuff is left in the den, I'm going to put it in this "big box," which will be kept out on the back porch. [spotlight your own action with a consequence]

TERRY: You have to be joking!

MRS. B: In addition, I've put new plastic bins in the kitchen for your schoolwork. [spotlight your own action] (She just couldn't bring herself to put school work in the big box.)

TERRY'S SISTER: *Why* are you doing this?

MRS. B: Now I won't be nagging, the den will be cleaned, and you won't need me to locate your missing stuff. You can find it yourself. [point out the benefit]

TERRY: Who cares anyway? How come you came up with this dumb idea?

MRS. B: Because school papers, an assortment of shoes and jackets, and other stuff are often left around the house. [state the facts without blame]

TERRY: It's not fair that you can do that with our stuff.

MRS. B: You, too, can put my stuff and Dad's stuff in the big box if it's left laying around. [set a house routine]

As you can see, Mrs. B avoided lecturing or preaching and used her words wisely. She also made a concrete change in the environment with the big box. But the most important part of her change is that she set up a situation that depended on *her* follow-through, no matter what anyone else did.

The big-box rule was not presented as a way to punish, to point the finger at one child, or to teach her kids a lesson. It was presented as a cooperative family effort that would bring more order to the household and would remove Mrs. B from the role of the lost and found department.

Would you believe this made an immediate change in the family? The den was clean, everyone retrieved their belongings and put them away, no one bothered Mom to find their stuff, and Mom spent the next ten years with lots more time for relaxing, reading the paper, and lingering over her coffee. Right? Guess again. Terry still uttered his famous "Where is my tennis shoe, Mom?" Often Mrs. B felt that Terry could trip over the big box and still not find his stuff. Even though she'd hoped Terry would change immediately, she came to realize that it would take time and, most important, consistency.

The person who *did* change immediately was Mom. Now,

instead of her usual response to Terry's desperate cries for help, she uttered these three words: "The big box." This was an important step in establishing a new routine in the household. If Terry and other family members weren't organized enough to put their stuff away consistently, at least they'd begin to take responsibility for locating their belongings. In addition, Terry's anger was redirected. Instead of yelling at Mom, he learned to get busy looking for his stuff, and eventually finding it. Best of all, Mrs. B didn't depend on Terry's immediate cooperation for encouragement. Instead, she was encouraged by her own change and by the fact that she had developed a rule with a follow-through that *she* carried out.

In the short run, Mrs. B achieved her goals of having an orderly household and stopping her fights with Terry about his belongings. In the long run, she did something more far-reaching. Because he was expected to locate his belongings at home, Terry was beginning to understand the concept of taking responsibility for his belongings in other areas as well. He was less likely to enlist his classmates and teacher in his frequent scavenger hunts to find his missing books, pencils, or homework assignments, which were usually camouflaged under a sea of papers. By talking less, changing the environment, and spotlighting her actions with consequences, Mrs. B was taking a step toward helping Terry make some generalized changes. He was learning to become more responsible for his belongings and ultimately more self-reliant in all areas of his life. And this was a valuable lesson indeed!

POINTS TO REMEMBER

1. Start to implement routines that involve your follow-through, rather than depend on your child's.

2. Let your child know ahead of time what is expected and what you will do. Don't spring the consequences on her. You're not trying to set your child up to experience consequences—you're trying to help her develop respect for routines and rules.

3. Present the consequence in a positive manner.

4. Your follow-through at home can pay off in a big way by impacting your child's approach to school, peer relationships, and ultimately his future.

5. Use the following communication skills when you follow up with follow-through:

* *Spotlight your own action with a consequence.*

* *Spotlight your own action.*

* *Point out the benefit.*

* *State the facts without blame.*

* *Set a house routine.*

Stay Grounded with Ground Rules

Stick to your nonnegotiable rules, and keep your credibility. You can stay grounded and keep your kids from breaking you down with their masterful use of logic and reason.

Now that you've learned the basics of setting up new routines, do you think your kid will just fall in line? Probably not. Your child will still put you and the routines to the test. All children test structure. That is part of their growing up—to evaluate, challenge, and ultimately develop their own ideas. Here is when parents are likely to cave in to the charm, demands, pleas, and persistence of their kids. Most parents don't even realize just how often they give up, give in, and reduce their credibility to zero. What can you do to avoid crumbling?

You can take a lesson from one mother, Mrs. S, who couldn't understand why her daughter, Zoe, didn't make a transition to the new rules and routine she had set up. Here's just one example of how Zoe worked the system and turned structure into mush.

At 6:00 one evening, Zoe and the neighbor's daughter, Meredith, were excitedly cooking up a plan. Zoe wanted to eat over and got the okay from Meredith's mom. Naturally, Zoe neglected to mention that her parents had just made a rule that Zoe could eat over at a friend's house one night a week and that she had already met her quota for that week. But that didn't stop her. She knew just how to proceed. She called her house, and Dad must have answered the phone, because Zoe kept insisting, "I want to speak to Mom." She wouldn't discuss the matter with Dad, and we can guess why. When Mom got on the phone, Zoe asked if she could eat at Meredith's. Mom obviously said no, because Zoe came up with one or two minor protests and then hung up. Immediately, as if she had never called, she picked up the phone again and called home. In fact, Zoe did this two more times. When the neighbor asked Zoe what she was doing, she confidently stated: "When I ask for something, I don't ask my dad, I ask my mom. But I have to ask three times before she says yes." Zoe knew the real rule— the rule that was never stated or admitted: "Never expect a yes on the first round, and never, never, let that stop you."

Mrs. S needed a way to prevent her daughter from swaying her with her well-thought-out reasons and justifications; she needed a way to avoid being led down the path of no return. She needed to learn to stay grounded in her rules and routines.

Soon enough, Zoe gave her mother another opportunity to stay grounded. Tuesday evening Zoe asked if her friend could sleep over. Mom and Dad said no as they reminded her of the house rule—no sleepovers on school nights. Of course, Zoe proceeded to whittle away mercilessly as she tried to get her way.

ZOE: Oh, *please!*

MRS. S: No, honey, tonight is a school night. We don't want you to have anyone sleep over. We want you to get to bed early.

ZOE: I promise, I promise. We'll go to bed early.

MRS. S: You have to write your spelling words out. Don't you have a spelling test tomorrow?

ZOE: We can help each other study. It'll be easier; we can test each other.

MRS. S: You can study on your own just as well.

ZOE: No, I can't. I want to study spelling with Meredith.

MRS. S: You better start listening to what I'm saying!

This kind of conversation goes nowhere. As Zoe promised, debated, pleaded, and whined, she also changed the subject. The discussion switched from sleepovers to doing homework with a friend. So far Mrs. S was not giving in, but she was inching toward a battle she would surely have liked to avoid.

Fortunately, Mrs. S didn't have to follow Zoe's lead from one topic to another. She didn't have to explain, reason, or defend herself. She could keep focused on her concern and her rule if she remembered to use the following skill:

"Stay Grounded" Statement

This jewel of a skill rescues parents from talking too much, getting off the subject, fighting, or giving in. Basically, the "stay grounded" statement is a simple verbal formula that you can hang on to when you feel yourself resorting to arguing, caving in, or just not following through.

When Zoe came up with her creative array of reasons, the conversation could have gone something like this:

MRS. S: There are no sleepovers on school nights.

ZOE: I promise, I promise, we will go to bed early.

MRS. S: I know you would go to bed early, and there are no sleepovers on school nights.

ZOE: We can help each other study. It'll be easier; we can test each other.

MRS. S: I know you could study together, and there are no sleepovers on school nights.

ZOE: I want to study spelling with Meredith.

MRS. S: I know you want to study spelling with Meredith, and there are no sleepovers on school nights.

As you can see, "stay grounded" statements are made up of three parts:

✳ *Summarizing calmly what your child said*

"I know you would go to bed early,

✳ *Using the word "and" to demonstrate that your child's feelings and your rule can coexist*

"and

✳ *Making a short statement repeating the rule*

"there are no sleepovers on school nights."

"Stay grounded" statements let you acknowledge your child's feelings while helping you stick to the point, validate your position, and send the message that "I mean what I say." The goal is not to completely squelch your child's persistence but to teach him to balance his tenacity with a healthy respect for others. Following through with reasonable rules at home helps kids accept limits elsewhere and channel their go-get-'em behavior into more constructive pursuits.

You will find an array of opportunities to use "stay grounded" statements. If your son comes up with a list of reasons why he does not want to go to Sunday school today—

"It's too early." "None of my friends go." "I don't like it."—you can acknowledge each reason, slip in that easy-to-forget "and," and then keep yourself grounded by repeating the basic rule. "It's time to go to Sunday school."

If your daughter lists several persuasive reasons why she can't walk the dog—"I'm on the phone." "I have too much homework." "It's cold out."—you can maintain your cool and your rule. Simply acknowledge each of her statements, use the connector "and," and repeat, "It's your turn to take out the dog." You should consider yourself successful if you

- stay "relatively" calm, even if your child doesn't, and avoid a major conflict

- stick to the subject

- show your child, and yourself, that you intend to be consistent

Whatever the issue, you can keep rules and routines going strong if you rely on "stay grounded" statements to keep from caving in. *The ability to stay grounded doesn't depend on your child's response, it depends on yours!*

POINTS TO REMEMBER

1. Don't cave in to your child's persistent maneuvers.

2. When you feel yourself losing ground, that's your cue that you're trying too hard to justify your position and convince your child you're right.

3. You can feel successful when you remain relatively calm, even if your child doesn't. Base your sense of success on *your* behavior, not your child's.

4. Stick to your guns by using "stay grounded" statements.

* *Summarize calmly what your child said.*

* *Use the word "and" to demonstrate that your child's feelings and your rule can coexist.*

* *Make a short statement repeating the rule.*

Quick Tip

Go for Negotiation

Create rules with your children, not just for them. They will be more likely to cooperate, and rules can be seen as positive tools to create order rather than a weapon used to clobber your kids.

Thus far we've discussed how parents can effectively implement structure in their households. The examples we've used have all been based on rules and routines set up by parents. Once parents have established the importance of structure, they can begin to involve their children in the process, because it is equally important for children to experience the value of creating routines, not just following them.

You will find that when your kids contribute to developing the order in the household, they have a much greater commitment to maintaining the established rules. How is this done? Through negotiation. When parents and children come together to problem-solve, everyone is heard and gets equal time. This is a perfect opportunity to get input from the entire family—including the kids.

Planning for Fun

Before you rush in to negotiate rules and routines with your kid, you can introduce the negotiation process as a way to plan fun family activities. This approach has several important purposes. First, and most obviously, it sets up fun family time as a routine. Second, because the topic is nonthreatening and full of fun, everyone can freely throw out ideas and hear what others have to say as they come up with a plan. Finally, while children are contributing to planning fun activities, they are learning the arts of brainstorming and negotiating. In the meantime, you are setting the stage for discussing other, more difficult issues.

So don't make the mistake of bringing up problems and complaints right away. Engage your children and get them enthusiastic about the negotiation process as you discuss a family vacation, plan the family activity for Sunday afternoon, or talk about where to go for a meal together. If you really want to get their attention, you could teach the negotiation process by using one of the most popular topics in most households—allowance.

Capitalizing on Your Kid's Love of Money

The word "allowance" is a surefire way to get kids of any age interested in the art of negotiating a routine—a routine of receiving money on a weekly basis. Rather than have money be a battle zone, you can actually capitalize on your kids' love of money as you use the routine of providing an allowance to teach the negotiation process.

An allowance is a wonderful gift to give a child. The gift is not the money but the sense of responsibility and empower-

ment it offers. A child can experience the good and bad decisions he has made. He can enjoy the feeling of finally saving
enough to get that particular baseball card he has been wanting
or suffer the disappointment of buying that prized toy that
turns out to be less than wonderful. When parents dole out
money according to their own whim or their children's wants,
children are deprived of the experience of saving and planning
ahead. Rather than learn about responsibility and sensible
spending, they learn about charming money out of Mom and
Dad.

But parents can set up a system that gives their children the
freedom and responsibility that come with the "Almighty Dollar." Whether it's fifty cents or five dollars, an allowance gives
a child a sense of independence and control over her life and
an opportunity to negotiate for herself.

Now let's see how parents and kids can best negotiate an
agreement. You will see soon enough that when it comes to
money the two biggest questions are How much? and What
for? How much money will your child get, and what items will
she be responsible for buying? Naturally, you should have
something specific in mind that you think is fair. But rather
than dictate your idea, you can invite your child to brainstorm
with you.

✳ *Invite Ideas*

"What do you think you'll need for an allowance?"

"How will you use your allowance?"

This is the starting-off point, when everyone's ideas get
presented. As you begin to move ahead, you will want to make
your expectations as clear as possible. You can do this by using
the following negotiation skill:

* "I'm Willing" and "I Want" Statements

"I'm willing *to give you $2.00 a week.*"

"I want *$1.00 of that to go into your piggy bank for saving.*"

"I'm willing *to give you $5.00 a week.*"

"I want *your extras like candy and movies with your friends to be your responsibility.*"

"I'm willing *to set up a $10.00 a week allowance.*"

"I want *your entertainment and school lunches to be your responsibility.*"

Notice, the key to this simple negotiation skill is to start with the "I'm willing" statement. When you begin by stating what you're willing to do, you're more likely to keep your child's attention and avoid locking horns. Then you can follow up with a statement about what you want in return. Be as clear and specific as you can, so there's little room for misunderstanding. As you practice this skill, your child will take his cues from you and begin stating what *he* wants and what *he* is willing to do—probably in just that order.

Because an allowance is such a good issue for negotiation, we'd now like to give you a few specific tips to bring with you to the "negotiating table."

Most parents want to know when they should start an allowance. One parent jokingly gave this rule of thumb: The best time to start an allowance is when your child starts "hounding" you mercilessly for candy as you go through the grocery store. Whether it's twenty-five cents for the gumball machine or fifty cents at the candy display near the checkout counter, this is your cue to begin an allowance. Then your child can select what she wants, and you can help her see how far she can stretch her money.

This is a far better time to start than when your child is a budding teenager and money is more likely to become a potential arena for fighting. If you want your child to be a savvy money manager, start him off at an early age.

As indicated in the "I'm willing, I want" examples, a child should know right from the beginning what he is expected to pay for. Setting up the purpose of an allowance beforehand makes it much easier to determine how much will be needed. It is interesting that when children are expected to pay for school lunches they magically begin making their own lunches so they can save their money for other things. This is a good example of a child beginning to set his priorities and budget his money.

As simple as it may seem, it is important to remember that an allowance belongs only to the child, and you must respect that. Many times parents vigorously nod their heads in agreement with this point while their hands are busily "borrowing" change from their kids' piggy banks. During one parent group meeting, a mother sheepishly reported that she borrowed her child's money rather regularly until the piggy bank was secretly removed, and her child calmly explained why. Another parent quickly chimed in with a topper to that story: "My oldest son never minded when I borrowed his change; he started charging me interest!" The point is it's your child's money, and she deserves some control over it.

Don't hold an allowance over a child's head by constantly threatening to withhold it every time she does something wrong. How many parents find themselves chanting this phrase throughout the week: "If you don't do this, you won't get your allowance"? Even when you are feeling most desperate, an allowance should not be a tool to control your child—it should be a tool to encourage independence. True, there will be occasions when you do withhold an allowance: for example, if a child has broken something and needs to pay for it or if a child is using money for illegal or harmful purposes. But by and large an allowance is something a child should be able to count on.

While an allowance is an issue that will surely hold your child's attention, you will also want to use negotiation to set up other routines that are not quite so interesting to your child. Household chores are a fine example of what we mean.

Assigning Household Chores

Making beds, cleaning up, doing dishes, and taking out the garbage occupy a great deal of our attention and time, especially when we're trying to get some help from our children. When you start chores at a young age kids want to help. They actually ask for things to do in the house. This is a good time to let family members write down chores on pieces of paper, put the papers in a job jar, and select a new chore each week.

So be sure to seize the early-on opportunity to teach your kid that every family member can contribute to household chores.

By the time your child reaches age seven or so, however, those glorious words "Mommy, can I help you?" are rarely volunteered. While job jars are great for young children, as kids get older they seem to "forget" to do their chores, or they want to be paid to do them.

One father, Mr. Y, was plagued by this problem with his two sons, Jeremy and Micah. Mr. Y was a staunch believer that kids should do chores because they are family members. Being a single parent, he had a lot of responsibility, and he was tired of doing most of the work around the house. He wanted more help. His sons were willing, but they wanted to make money. Jeremy had his eye on a new baseball glove, and Micah was determined to save up for one of those big cassette players. They figured the best way to increase their cash flow would be to do chores around the house.

Mr. Y didn't go for it. "Parents don't get paid for chores. Why should kids?" he said, as he complained to us of his plight. He didn't feel guilty—after all, he was no tyrant, and he was not asking for something outrageous. Besides, his boys had some money; he did give them an allowance every week. The least they could do was pull their fair share of the work around the house.

What did Mr. Y do? He decided to go for negotiation in the hope that together he and his sons could come up with a solution that each of them could live with. During one of our family counseling sessions, he got the ball rolling by encouraging some brainstorming:

"The chores are not getting done. What do you think we can do about it?" [invite ideas]

These boys weren't dummies. They did what they could to keep the conversation from moving ahead. They just sat there tight-lipped.

That didn't stop Mr. Y. He made his point in a clear and reasonable manner by using "I'm willing" and "I want" statements.

"I'm willing to do some of the household chores."

"I want help with some routine chores."

Did the boys jump right in and agree to help out? No. But they did begin a little negotiating of their own. They weren't ready to give up the idea of extra cash. Back and forth it went until they finally came up with a surprisingly reasonable idea:

The kids would help with "routine" chores—setting the table, walking the dog, emptying the dishwasher, and taking out the garbage—and they would not get paid. They would rotate their chores and even built some added flexibility into the process by including the options of trading and bartering. For example, Mr. Y could trade his taking out the garbage for Jeremy's dog walking when Jeremy had a late baseball practice.

The boys did get something more than helping with chores out of this deal. While they agreed to do regular household chores without pay, they would get paid for extra jobs, such as cutting the lawn, shoveling snow, washing windows, vacuuming the family room, and cleaning out the garage.

The proposal seemed reasonable to Mr. Y, and the boys realized this was probably as good as it was going to get. There was only one problem they had not yet tackled. What would happen if the regular chores didn't get done? Before the Y family left, we suggested that they seal the deal by setting up a consequence.

Here's where the family rose to the occasion—they came

up with a host of possible consequences that sealed the deal.

> MR. Y: If the chores of the day aren't done by 10:00 P.M.,
> then I'll do them, charging $2.00 per chore.
>
> *Or*
>
> MR. Y: If someone forgets to do the chore, he has to do it
> immediately and also has to do it an extra day.
>
> *Or*
>
> MICAH: If I end up having to do one of your chores, then
> you'll have to do one of mine.

This final discussion highlights an important skill in the negotiating process, the commitment to "seal the deal." Once you've invited ideas, and compromised with an "I'm willing, I want" statement, you may need to add this third negotiation skill. Once the consequence is established, it should be stated in as clear and specific a manner as possible, so there are no surprises. In this case, the Y family was able to seal the deal with a consequence that everyone could at least tolerate. What they ultimately decided upon is not as important as the fact that there were many options and no one right answer. The Y family chose what worked for them, just as your family will choose what will work for you.

For Mr. Y the best part was, "Everyone made sure the rule was followed. The boys thought the rule was fair, and they knew exactly what was expected of them. They kept themselves in line much better than I could."

In addition to the actual decisions made about these chores, Jeremy and Micah came away with something even more lasting and perhaps more important: the skills of brainstorming, problem solving, compromising, and the ability to state their ideas as well as hear the ideas of others—even when they didn't agree. These are the skills they'll carry with them into relationships with friends and with teachers. These are the skills that will help them communicate with people and approach life tasks with a problem-solving attitude.

POINTS TO REMEMBER

1. Remember that children need to learn how to create rules and routines, not just follow them.

2. Use this process to discuss subjects that interest your kid, like vacation plans, allowances, and purchases, not just problems or rules.

3. Include everyone involved in your negotiations. You'll be surprised at how even the youngest child can come up with the perfect solution.

4. Keep your negotiating short and to the point so you avoid preaching and blaming.

5. Don't bring something up for discussion if you really don't want your kid's input on it. If something is nonnegotiable, present it as just that.

6. Use the following communication skills to negotiate with your child:

✻ Invite ideas.

✻ Make "I'm willing" and "I want" statements.

✻ Seal the deal with a consequence.

Build
Responsibility

We have just discussed how parents can set up structure in their households—structure that reduces chaos and teaches children some valuable long-range skills. Parents, however, do not simply want to train their kids to be compliant little rule followers. Sure, there are going to be times when you may think that's exactly what you'd like, but that's no preparation for the years to come. The challenge for you is to take the natural independence that can often breed conflict and use it to move your child toward responsibility and self-reliance. While no parent would argue with this goal, parents often unknowingly make it more difficult than need be. Without meaning to they set up countless scenarios where independence is used as a threat or punishment. They may say,

> *"If you don't get downstairs right now, you'll just have to* get your own cereal *for breakfast."*

> *"If you don't stop bothering me, you'll have to* make your own lunch *for school."*

> *"You better undress faster than that or you'll have to* take a bath by yourself."

These remarks send a message to your child that self-reliance becomes necessary when you're too angry to help her. Children learn to associate independence with occasions when Mom and Dad are too irritated to help rather than to see it as an accomplishment. The tasks of making one's own breakfast, packing one's own lunch, taking a bath by oneself, and other opportunities for responsibility need to be presented in a positive manner. Parents need to learn to use these and other daily opportunities for self-reliance as their chance to build independence in a casual and natural way. And when parents do present these chances for independence many will delight over their children's take-charge attitude. While it's true that some children will tackle becoming good self-managers with ease, there will always be those who fight the parents' urging toward self-reliance. Even when parents try to be positive the child may lack confidence, feel overwhelmed, or may simply be stubborn. Whatever the reason for a child's reluctance to accept responsibility for self-management, parents often see any unwillingness as evidence of uncooperative, spiteful behavior, and they respond by pushing even harder. Rather than push, a parent can address the child's reluctance and still move him toward independence. He can start teaching self-reliance by using the following three approaches:

- Turn tasks into tidbits.
- Keep your kid in the director's chair.
- Treat 'em as a team.

Each of these techniques gives you the tools to remain supportive and provide guidance while you encourage independence and self-reliance.

Turn Tasks into Tidbits

Ensure a feeling of success by cutting in-dependent tasks into manageable bite-size pieces. You can start with the young child, small decisions, and small responsibilities. Rather than focus on important, over-whelming issues, use the seemingly insig-nificant activities that fill every child's day.

Turning tasks into tidbits is merely the art of breaking down tasks into small step-by-step pieces that the child can tackle with confidence. When we discuss breaking down tasks, our experience is that parents' attention turns im-mediately to somewhat complex, demanding tasks, such as managing money or doing school projects that require a lot of preparation. Children clearly benefit from breaking down these types of tasks into more manageable pieces; however, we sug-gest that you begin to use this process with small, seemingly insignificant tasks that are often taken for granted. By starting with small tasks, you make independence a nonthreatening learning process that maximizes your child's sense of success and minimizes the battle of wills that results when a child feels pushed or threatened. Therefore, we suggest that you begin this process with benign, nonconflictual opportunities for inde-pendence.

To demonstrate, here is an example of one unsuspecting mother, Mrs. T, who sincerely expected her daughter to happily embrace a chance to act independently. Was she in for a surprise!

Early one evening, when Tessie looked like she was badly in need of a bath and her mother, Mrs. T, was moving at her usual busy pace, Mrs. T decided this would be a convenient time for Tessie to start taking a bath by herself. Delighted with the idea, Mom filled the tub and then uttered a sentence that she never dreamed would stir up an argument: "You have to take your bath now." Tessie refused.

As Mrs. T began to get fed up, her calm asking moved to insisting and threatening. Tessie reluctantly undressed. Just as Mrs. T thought they were on their way to victory, Tessie refused to wash herself. "I can't do this by myself," she cried. Mrs. T knew Tessie was quite capable of doing it herself, but she didn't have the energy to fight. The scenario ended with Mom washing Tessie, all the while complaining that Tessie should be washing herself. This could hardly be called a fun and cooperative atmosphere that encourages independent behavior.

What happened was that Tessie took a simple task and turned it into a major aggravation. Instead of having bathtime be an argument, Mrs. T could have used this nonthreatening, simple task as a tool to teach responsibility gradually despite Tessie's resistance.

Instead of simply handing over responsibility as Mrs. T did, you can turn things around by breaking even this simplest opportunity for self-management into bite-size pieces—by turning tasks into tidbits. We will use Mrs. T's bathtime battle to illustrate the four-stage process that increases cooperation as you move your child toward self-reliance.

Stage 1: Getting the Job Done

In stage 1, you do the job entirely, taking full responsibility, while you teach your child. As you direct, involve your child in limited ways and gain his commitment. This can be done simply by offering the child a choice between two agreeable options. In our example, rather than approach Tessie with the statement "Tessie, you have to take your bath now"—a remark that might well result in "No, I want to finish watching my TV show"—Mrs. T could have involved Tessie in a basic yet positive way by using the following:

✳ *Give 'Em a Voice in Their Choice*

"Would you like your bath now or after that TV program?"

Quite simply, you offer your child a choice between two options while continuing to take charge of the outcome. This is a way to turn over a decision to a child while still providing guidance and structure.

Here are a few more examples of how you can involve your child at this stage:

"Are you going to write your thank-you note tonight or Saturday morning?"

"Are you going to finish cleaning the basement now or after you go bike riding?"

To be truly effective, you should remember two key points when you offer a limited choice:

1. Be specific, and offer choices that you're willing to accept. Don't fall into the trap of trying to convince your

child to do what you'd prefer, after he's already chosen something else. This will teach the child that his choices and judgments are "wrong" unless they coincide with yours.

2. Don't confuse warning or putting the squeeze on your child with offering a choice. "Either take your bath now or you can't watch TV." "Either be quiet or go to your room." "You can buy this toy or nothing at all." may be appropriate from time to time, but these are not the kinds of choices that develop decision-making skills.

Stage 2: The Cooperative Effort

As soon as possible, you can move to stage 2 and give your child some of the responsibility for completing the task. The secret is to offer it in a way that keeps you and your kid cooperating while you avoid the role of "boss." It's easy, if you remember this skill:

* Inject an Idea without Being a Bully

In Mrs. T's case, instead of saying,

"You have to get everything ready while the bath is filling up. Get your clean clothes, washcloth, towel, and don't forget the shampoo. You have to wash your hair."

try the following:

"Why don't you bring the things you'll need, like clothes, washcloth, towel, and shampoo, into the bathroom while the tub is filling?"

By introducing questions with the words "Why don't you . . ." you can gently motivate your child to take the initiative without demanding that he do so. You are giving your child a slight push toward taking care of himself in small ways. If the child does not take your suggestion, he is not opposing a demand, and there is not a likelihood for conflict.

When you can inject an idea without being a bully, you can offer ideas that encourage your child to begin to take the initiative. Here are three further examples of what we mean:

> "Why don't you *call the store to ask if they have those shoes in your size?"*
>
> "Why don't you *check the paper to see if there are any good sales on the bike you want?"*
>
> "Why don't you *check the school phone book for that telephone number you need?"*

"Why don't you" is a phrase to keep in your back pocket and pull out whenever the opportunity arises. And here's an extra tip: Whenever appropriate, you can use this skill to suggest that your child complete a task. It is very encouraging to let the child do the final step, because this gives him a sense of accomplishment.

Stage 3: Stand by Me

In stage 3, your child does the task from beginning to end while you "stand by." In the case of Tessie, Mrs. T could have sat back and watched as Tessie took a bath. Here's where parents often utter *a few* encouraging comments: "I notice how well you washed your feet." "You are doing a great job." That's fine. But remember, you don't need to go overboard with compliments. Your ultimate goal is to remove yourself as the audience and keep your child from holding you hostage longer than necessary.

Remember, while your approval is important, you want to teach your child to rely on himself, not you, for constant reinforcement. With this in mind, you can see that this stage is a wonderful time to make comments that encourage self-evaluation, not just reliance on your evaluation. Children need to learn to value their own ability and appraisal of themselves, and they can gain this confidence when you use the following:

* Self-Evaluation Questions

"*Aren't you pleased with yourself?*"

"*What did you learn from that?*"

"*What did you think of the way that worked out?*"

"*How do you think you're doing?*"

These questions are thought provokers and provide good opportunities for children to pat themselves on the back.

However, we want to state one note of caution. Don't drag this stage out longer than necessary, or you may find yourself stuck in it, like one well-meaning mother, Mrs. O. She related the fact that even after her daughter had managed the task of bathing herself she was unwilling to give up her mother's company in the bathroom.

Her daughter Shelby so enjoyed Mom standing by captive as she took her bath and chatted about the day's events that she wouldn't let her go. Shelby had turned her bath routine into her special time alone with Mom. Mom felt guilty about refusing this "special time," especially when her daughter said, "I'll do everything—you just sit there and relax." Of course to "encourage" Mom to stay and visit, she added remarks like "You haven't spent enough time with me today." For three years this mom had special time in the bathroom with her daughter, until Mrs. O went out of town for a week. When she returned, her daughter had miraculously managed to start showering without company. Needless to say, Mrs. O never again even went near the bathroom when her daughter was there.

Stage 4: Turn Over the Task

In the final stage, you've reached your goal. Your child does the entire task by himself. In Tessie's case, she would take her bath alone while Mom was in a different room. Sometimes, when a child finally takes over, he may not do the task just as Mom or Dad would like. Still, if at all possible, you should fight the urge to rush in and take over. Instead, use the following two skills together:

* State Your Thoughts or Feelings

and

* Show Faith in Your Child

"I thought this would be a good day to wash your hair, [state your thoughts or feelings]

"but you know your schedule best so I'm sure you'll find a good time." [show faith in your child]

"I'm a little unsure that five minutes in the tub is all that's needed, [state your thoughts or feelings]

"but I have to remind myself that you know how much time you need." [show faith in your child]

Remember, the goal is to develop your child's sense of independence and ability, not to have your child do the task perfectly.

Thus far we've seen how you can use this step-by-step process over a relatively short period of time on rather simple

tasks. If you start with small decisions while your child is young, your child is less likely to balk as responsibilities become more difficult and the tasks more demanding. But don't limit your use of this process to simple tasks. These steps are also very effective for teaching all kinds of responsibilities, even those that are mastered over years.

To illustrate this point, let's look at a task that greets every parent and child as each September rolls around—shopping for school supplies. Usually parents and kids do this task together, as parents clutch that list of supplies to make sure the items are checked off. Parents would love to see their children eagerly shop for the "right" folder, the "right" lined paper. What happens instead? The parent picks out the school supplies while the kid is wandering toward the toy or candy department. "What about this folder? How wide does the lined paper have to be?" screams the parent as she searches for her child. Typically Mom and Dad fail to get it all quite right. "Mom, I can't use the five-ring notebook, it has to be three rings." "I don't want a blue binder; I wanted red." "Dad, those pencils aren't the fat kind that are easier to write with." And so it goes, until a parent grits her teeth. "What is the difference?" "Just get this; it will do." Or the ultimate threat, "Do it yourself."

Rather than wait until you're faced with this frustrating scenario, keep your eye on the future, and start training your child now. Here's how you can apply the four-stage process to school supply shopping madness—or, for that matter, any kind of shopping.

Stage 1: Getting the Job Done

Take responsibility for the task of shopping, while giving your child limited choices.

"Would you like to get the red mat for rest or the blue one?"
[give 'em a voice in their choice]

Stage 2: The Cooperative Effort

Begin to teach your child to take some initiative.

"Why don't you call the store before we go to see if it has the right kind of binders?" [inject an idea without being a bully]

"Why don't you check off the items on the list as we get each one?" [inject an idea without being a bully]

Stage 3: Stand by Me

This stage probably doesn't happen until a child is eight or nine. Now you can step back and let your child take more responsibility for the shopping. It's your child who will run around the store hunting for that perfect pencil holder, while you act as helper and set some limits regarding budget. You can encourage your child with compliments, but remember that your approval should be secondary to your child's self-evaluation.

"Aren't you pleased with your selections?" [ask self-evaluation questions]

"What did you learn by comparing those prices?" [ask self-evaluation questions]

"Aren't you proud of how far you stretched that $10.00?" [ask self-evaluation questions]

Stage 4: Turn Over the Task

Finally, your child can be on his own. You can drop him off at the store or mall to buy the supplies with his list in hand. Once your child is in charge of a purchase, it's up to you to stay out of it. Yes, you can give an opinion, but when the urge to say "Are you kidding, how could you spend money on that?" creeps in, fight it, and instead say something like this:

> *"I wouldn't have thought you'd need such a fancy note-book, [state your thoughts or feelings]*

> *"but you know what you need better than I do." [show faith in your child]*

You will use these four stages differently to meet your child's individual needs. Some children tend to be more cautious, less comfortable doing even simple tasks independently, while others push their parents' "help" away. Some tasks require a lot of parental supervision, while others are less complicated and can be easily managed by a child. The point is that these four stages provide a process that any parent can adapt. And it is a process that not only helps a reluctant child but also helps the reluctant parent who just can't seem to let go.

In truth, turning tasks into tidbits is a wonderful framework for children and parents as you work together toward your child's gradual independence. By breaking tasks down into four manageable stages, you are structuring success. You can compliment your child on the good job she has done as you continue to teach and guide her.

By encouraging independence through simple and eventually more demanding tasks, you give your child a chance to test his ability to consider options and make decisions with little risk. Even though it may be a little inconvenient at times, take advantage of these unlimited opportunities for "practice runs." They will ultimately prepare your child to tackle more difficult situations. The more practice he has, the more he will trust his own judgment and, of utmost importance, feel in control of his life.

So start with the simple areas, where you've got the best chance for success, and build your way up to the more challenging tasks of life. Then watch how making choices, taking initiative, and becoming independent will become a part of your kid's life in all areas.

POINTS TO REMEMBER

1. Start to encourage independence with small, every-day tasks. They are the building blocks for future independence.

2. If your child seems fearful or unwilling to take responsibility, teach him gradually by breaking the task down into four manageable stages.

3. As your child becomes accomplished at completing tasks on her own, teach her to rely on herself, not on you, for constant approval.

4. When you turn tasks into tidbits, use the following communication skills:

   * *Give 'em a voice in their choice. (Stage 1)*

   * *Inject an idea without being a bully. (Stage 2)*

   * *Ask self-evaluation questions. (Stage 3)*

   * *State your thoughts or feelings. (Stage 4)*

   * *Show faith in your child. (Stage 4)*

Quick Tip

Keep Your Kid in the Director's Chair

Try to avoid taking over your kids'
responsibilities no matter how hard they
try to get you involved. Balance your
decision to hand responsibility back with a
supportive, caring attitude.

By turning tasks into tidbits, we have seen how you can begin to turn over small responsibilities and limited decisions to foster your child's initiative and self-reliance. But what about those occasions when you don't have the luxury of time on your side, occasions when your child has responsibilities that have to be handled *now?* You can learn to prod your child toward independence as you pry yourself away from the process. You can learn to let your child remain in charge while you remain supportive. To illustrate this point, we will turn to an area that highlights the issue of responsibility and self-management in many households—homework.

Naturally, parents must always investigate whether children's reluctance to do homework is the result of a learning problem and, if so, get appropriate help. But we often find that even the most capable of children can be quite skillful at overly involving their parents in school assignments as they try to take the pressure off themselves.

Here's an example of one parent, Mrs. R, who found herself in this very predicament with her son, Larry.

* * *

Larry's teacher had given the class a genealogy assignment. Each child had to choose a family member to interview and write about. When Mrs. R first heard of this project she said, "What a great idea!" But by the time Larry got done asking his mom "to help," she wished she'd never heard the word "genealogy." Here's how she recounted Larry's rather persistent attempt to get her to take over the responsibility for his project:

LARRY: I have this really hard genealogy project for school. I have to interview someone in my family. Who do you think I should call?

MRS. R: "You could ask Grandpa. He loves to talk. Or Aunt Phyllis will be in town next week, and I know she'd love to help you.

LARRY: Mom, I just want to get it done!

MRS. R: What do you mean you just want to get it done!

LARRY: Maybe Grandpa would be good. (And without missing a beat, he added:) Will you call him?

MRS. R: You should be the one making that call.

LARRY: I just can't. I don't know what to say.

MRS. R: First you tell him about the project. Then you start with some simple questions like "Where were you born? When did you move to this country?"

LARRY: Will you do it, *please?*

Mrs. R said that the more she tried to remove herself from the task, the more Larry baited her with questions and pleas. She knew she should not jump in and do the assignment, but what *should* she do? Should she have removed herself from the project altogether and told Larry he was on his own? No. That kind of abrupt withdrawal is likely to escalate into an argument, as Larry tries even harder to keep Mom involved with comments like "You don't care if I fail! Everyone else's parents help them with hard work."

Many of you would have little sympathy, even if Larry became more and more upset. "What's so terrible about the child being upset, especially when he's trying to avoid his work?" you might ask. The issue is not whether Larry is upset.

The issue is this: *When parents withdraw in anger, they often set up a scenario in which their children lose sight of the task and quickly become absorbed in how uncaring, mean, and generally terrible the parents are.* That's when a child latches on to the notion that he is a victim, and an innocent victim at that. The child forgets about his problems as he zeros in on fighting with the "awful, immovable parent."

To avoid this outcome, Mrs. R needed to find a balance between being helpful and refusing to take over the job. Ultimately, she needed to find a way to remain supportive while firmly but gently letting Larry struggle with the assignment instead of struggling with her. Here's a series of statements Mrs. R, or any parent, might use to ease herself away from the task and from a potential argument too:

LARRY: I have this really hard genealogy project for school. I have to interview someone in my family. Who do you think I should call?

MRS. R: Hmmm. Let me think a moment. When do you need it finished? Do you have a lot of time to work on it?

LARRY: I just want to get it done soon!

MRS. R: Knowing that your goal is just to get it done soon, who do you think you'll interview?

LARRY: Maybe Grandpa would be good. Will you call him?

MRS. R: I'll stay and listen as you call Grandpa from the kitchen phone.

LARRY: What should I ask him?

MRS. R: I don't know.

LARRY: Well, I don't know either!

MRS. R: Why don't you come up with the questions before you call him? It might be easier that way.

LARRY: I can't think of any.

MRS. R: Then you really made a good choice with Grandpa, because he loves to talk. You probably won't need to ask a lot of questions.

We call the techniques in this conversation "hand-it-back" skills. They are the communication skills that keep your child in the role of director while you maintain a supportive role. They are the skills that keep you from getting hooked by a persistent child and instead send the message, in a loud, clear, but kind way, "It's up to you." While it is not necessary to use all six "hand-it-back" skills at any given time, it's helpful to acquaint yourself with them and know how to use them in a way that seems comfortable to you and appropriate to the situation. Here's an explanation of them.

✻ Pinpoint the Goal

"Hmmm. Let me think a moment. When do you need it finished? Do you have a lot of time to work on it?"

While it's okay to make a suggestion, it's more important to encourage a child to pinpoint her own specific goals, such as meeting a deadline or coming up with a particular idea. Note, you should have your child choose the goal rather than tell him how to proceed toward a goal *you* have selected.

"How soon do you need to get started?"

is quite different from

"You better start this assignment soon or you'll never get it done."

Here are three additional examples of pinpointing the goal:

"What is your target date for that project?"

"What part in the play have you decided to try out for?"

"What grade are you shooting for on the math test?"

* Turn Over the Responsibility

"Knowing that your goal is just to get it done soon, who do you think you'll interview?"

This type of comment lets your child know the responsibility is hers. Instead of preaching, directing, or rescuing by taking care of the problem, you should let your child know it is up to her to make the decision or solve the problem. This is the kind of comment you can use when you feel your child has just dangled the bait and you don't want to get hooked.

Here are three additional comments you can use to turn over the responsibility:

"What do you think you should do about it?"

"I wonder which way you'll decide to go."

"I'll be anxious to see how it works out."

* Offer Support

"I'll stay and listen as you call Grandpa from the kitchen phone."

Offering support is an important skill. It is your chance to show your willingness to help without taking over. If you feel your child needs more than support—needs some concrete help—make sure the child gives you a limited, specific task. You want to help your child in a way that keeps her as the director and you as the assistant. Here are three comments that will both offer support and keep your role in check:

> *"How can I be helpful?"*

> *"I have about fifteen minutes free now. Is there* anything in particular *you want me to do?"*

> *"When you figure out what* specific *thing I can help with, let me know."*

* Don't Be a Know-it-all

> *"I don't know."*

Who says you have to know all the answers? Sometimes you are better off not wracking your brain to figure out the perfect answer for your kid. It's not just that you're depriving your child of the challenge; it's that—more often than we'd like to think—our kids come up with better solutions or answers than we do.

Here are two additional comments that will let your kids know you don't always know all the answers:

> *"I wish I knew how to help you, but I'm not sure what to do."*

> *"I'm not sure where to start either."*

* Inject an Idea without Being a Bully

"Why don't you *come up with the questions before you call him? It might be easier that way.*"

As we've already seen, using "why don't you" questions allows you to offer an idea to your child without being demanding. You can implicitly suggest an idea that might help your child take action, and at the same time leave the decision to her. Remember, this is not a time to tell your child what she should do. It is a time to simply and briefly offer some suggestions in an encouraging manner.

Here are two additional examples of how to inject an idea without being a bully:

"Why don't you call your classmates to borrow the book you forgot?"

"Why don't you ride your bike to soccer practice today so you don't have to wait for us?"

* Show Faith in Your Child

"You really made a good choice with Grandpa, because he loves to talk. You probably won't need to ask a lot of questions."

As we've already suggested, it's important to show faith in your child even when you may have handled a situation differently. This is especially true if your child is taking the easiest way out. And if you can't say something with at least some honesty, it's best not to try. Remember, however, that what's important is not how a child chooses to handle one particular situation. The important issue is that you are supporting the process of independent decision making.

*   *   *

Here are two additional statements you can make to show some faith:

> *"I know you'll do what's right for you."*
>
> *"I really think you can work this out."*

It's important to use any of these skills with a loving, caring tone. This is no place for sarcasm. You are not challenging your child; you are not setting her up to do something on her own to fail. You are encouraging her self-management skills while remaining supportive. These thought-provoking kinds of statements can help any child explore different options and feel encouraged to solve problems. You can use these comments to teach your child to motivate herself with her own ideas, goals, and expectations. So avoid getting hooked into the role of director or savior as you give your child that gentle but important push toward learning to manage her own life.

Keep an Open Mind

As parents, we will quickly notice that when children create their own options, set goals, and make decisions, they won't always do exactly as we would like. They may not do a school project the way we think they should; they may decide to spend their allowance on something we don't value. Therefore, just as we teach our children to broaden their options, we must broaden our own options so we can be as open as possible to our children's "creative" ideas. Children need to find their own way without feeling pressured to do things *our* way.

Here's an example of how one mom and dad learned to keep an open mind and appreciate how their son turned his aversion to physical labor into a profitable, fun, and tasty experience.

Scott was involved in a fund-raising event through Boy Scouts. Every year his troop raised money to donate to a shelter. Most of the kids in his group followed the "suggestions" offered by their den leader. They went around the neighborhood looking for work mowing lawns and cleaning garages. This was completely unappealing to Scott, who, according to his father, relished relaxing more than any other child he knew. This child knew the true meaning of leisure time, and his parents felt this need to avoid work was really getting in the way of an important commitment. They found themselves feeling angry as Scott deftly avoided their suggestions for earning money. The more they "suggested," the less Scott listened.

However, Scott surprised them with an enterprising idea. Faced with the need to make money and the commitment to avoid physical labor as much as possible, Scott came up with a plan that met both his criteria. He got permission to set up a table in his little sister's classroom on Father's Night. That's the evening dads come to school with their kids to look at their artwork and other projects. He had his mom take him to the grocery store and front him some money. He chose two flavors of ice cream and two kinds of toppings. He used plastic spoons and cups from home. On the big night, he packed up his goodies in a cooler and was in business—ice cream sundaes for $1.50. Scott knew that once one little kid got one the rest were a shoo-in, because what dad would say no to an ice cream sundae on Father's Night! Scott had come up with a great idea to raise money and at the same time had fun eating ice cream as he was doing it. He used his ability to make choices, initiate a plan, and follow through, and his parents were beginning to develop some appreciation for Scott's ingenious ideas.

*   *   *

Scott was able to meet the goal; he simply chose a different path than what was expected. What about the times a child not only takes a different path but ends up with a result you aren't prepared for? That's the real test of parents' ability to keep an open mind and perhaps put themselves in their children's shoes. This is particularly true when the parent in question is a family therapist who prides herself on encouraging independence and responsibility, as in the following case.

Mrs. F had just gotten off the phone. "We're all invited to the Zinns' house for dinner," she announced.

Her two girls were excited. They always had fun at the Zinns' playing with their two daughters. Mrs. F's son, Seth, definitely did not share their enthusiasm. "Girls," he said. "All they have is a bunch of girls. I hate going there."

Mrs. F tried to point out some of the positive aspects, which she had to admit she really had to stretch for. But Seth held his ground, insisting it would be a horrible evening for him. He hated the Zinns' "girl toys"; he'd have nothing to do; the girls wouldn't let him play with them, and on and on. Mom could not move Seth one inch. When she felt she'd exhausted every avenue, she said, "We're all going. I am not canceling out because you don't like playing with the girls." That was that—she thought.

Seth responded with, "What if I can find something else to do?"

"Fine," said Mrs. F.

However, this was not the kind of "fine" that means "Okay dear." It was the kind of "fine" that means "I'm tired of discussing this; there are no options; you're going."

Ten minutes later Seth came downstairs with a big smile. "Well, I made plans. I'm eating at Brent's and playing at his house until you get home. I explained the whole situation, and his mom said it would be 'fine.'"

Mrs. F had not anticipated this twist in plans, and her first inclination was to tell Seth he shouldn't have invited himself to his friend's house. However, she stopped and thought about it for a moment. She had said he could do something else—even though she hadn't meant it—and, quite honestly, she had never seen Seth move that fast to take care of anything. She was pretty impressed. Seth took her by surprise, and his ingenuity forced her to be true to her word.

Naturally, there will be some areas where you draw the line and insist that something be done "your way." But we encourage you to limit these areas to the very important issues. On the less important issues, try to keep an open mind and enjoy watching your child problem-solve. If you can't enjoy it, at least keep quiet and remember the long-range goals of helping your child broaden her own options, develop some creative problem-solving strategies, and take responsibility for managing her life.

POINTS TO REMEMBER

1. When you feel yourself getting drawn into taking over your child's responsibility, stand firm and continue to hand back the responsibility.

2. Whenever possible, balance your refusal to solve your child's problem with willingness to help in some small, specific way.

3. Avoid blaming and battling. Your goal is to get your child busy struggling with the problem at hand rather than struggling with you.

4. Keep an open mind, even when your child's solution is not one you would have chosen. Your long-range goal is to help your child develop creative problem-solving strategies and manage her own life.

5. Use your own combination of the following six "hand-it-back" skills to hand responsibility back to your child in a caring manner:

>   * *Pinpoint the goal.*
>
>   * *Turn over the responsibility.*
>
>   * *Offer support.*
>
>   * *Don't be a know-it-all.*
>
>   * *Inject an idea without being a bully.*
>
>   * *Show faith in your child.*

Quick Tip

Treat 'Em as a Team

Sibling relationships are a great place to teach your kids to be cooperative team players. So during sibling fights, instead of dividing your kids or showing favoritism by taking sides, unite your kids and encourage them to problem-solve and learn important relationship skills.

By turning tasks into tidbits and keeping your child in the director's chair and by keeping an open mind, you help your child develop skills in independence and self-reliance. As you gradually turn over responsibilities to your child, she learns to use her own resources to take care of a wide range of tasks and problems. Now you are ready to rise to the ultimate challenge—and deal with a most difficult area of encouraging self-reliance. You are ready to begin to encourage independence in relationships, and the best place to start is sibling relationships.

Don't worry, we're not going to suggest you let them "go at it." What we can do, though, is show you ways to intervene that will take the responsibility for working things out off your shoulders and put it where it surely belongs, onto your kids. With practice and guidance, children can learn to work out many of their differences without making their fights into a three-ring circus with you as the ringmaster.

Parents don't enjoy running interference every time their kids get into a fight, so why do so many of us do it? Because we are operating under two misguided principles. First, we believe our children shouldn't fight, they should love each other, or at least get along. We all hope that our kids will learn to love each other, but it's not very likely that they will always get along. Just as parents have the right to argue with each other without outside interference, children should have the right to air their differences. Our job is not to stop sibling fighting altogether but to decrease its frequency and its impact on family life. Second, we believe we must, above all, provide justice. We move into the arena of sibling battles armed with reason, a multitude of solutions, and often, above all, the commitment to be fair.

It was that commitment to be fair that kept one mom, Mrs. V, on her toes and in her kids' fights on an all too regular basis.

Somehow all Mrs. V's attempts at creating peace and goodwill just weren't working. As soon as one dispute was settled, another cropped up to take its place. It wasn't that she enjoyed her role as peacemaker; in fact, she was rather sick of it. But she didn't know what else to do. When her kids would utter that battle cry "It's not fair," like many parents, Mrs. V saw it as her cue to get involved. Mrs. V recounted one very typical scenario to a group of parents. As she described the scene, parents in the room shook their heads in agreement, as if to say, "That's just what happens in my house." See if this dialogue sounds familiar to you.

ALEX: Johnny took the Legos I needed to finish this building.

JOHNNY: It's not fair. He has more than me, and I was playing with them first.

MRS. V (ADDRESSING ALEX): Is that true? Was Johnny first?

ALEX: No, we started at the same time, plus Johnny pinched my arm when I went to get more Legos. Look how red it is.

JOHNNY: No, I didn't.

MRS. V: I'm sure he didn't mean to hurt you. He's upset because he wants to make something nice like you did. Johnny, you know you're not supposed to pinch. If you're angry, use your words.

JOHNNY: He pushed me first and made me fall and hurt myself.

Now, to be truly fair, what did Mrs. V try to do? Like any good judge, she tried to get all the facts and find out what really happened.

"Is that true? Was Johnny first?"

Naturally, each of her children was more than willing to cooperate and give her as many "facts" as he could muster to show just how wrong the other one was.

She also tried to point out the instigator's good points to get the angry child to change his mind.

"I'm sure he didn't mean to hurt you. He's upset because he wants to build something nice like you did."

While these attempts may seem to work in the short run, they don't work over the long haul. Rather than teaching a child how to cooperate and problem-solve with her sibling, these comments teach a child to depend on someone else to arbitrate, rescue, and settle squabbles. They also teach the child to make herself look good at her sibling's expense as she proclaims her innocence and points out the misbehavior of her "creepy" sister. Instead of promoting cooperation, these attempts promote competition.

What can parents do when they want to intervene? Instead of questioning, reasoning, rationalizing, or minimizing, they can treat 'em as a team.

The treat 'em as a team approach plays up the notion of mutual responsibility and plays down the possibility of favoritism or proclaiming which sibling is good and which is bad. It is an approach that treats the kids as equals so they will begin to respect each other as equals. Does this mean that you have to go through parenthood measuring every cookie, every present, every ounce of free time? Absolutely not. Don't confuse the concept of treating your children as a team with the notion of treating your children equally all of the time. *Each child has different needs at different times, and it's a parent's job to address those different needs, not to split the world into equal parts for each kid.* Children deserve and need special, individualized attention. At different times they will need different amounts of time, help, attention, and so forth. As parents, we have to remember that our job is not to worry about what is equal or fair; our job is to provide what our children need. The treat 'em as a team approach does not ignore individual needs; it is a tool parents can use that can help them avoid blaming, taking sides, or playing judge during sibling fights.

What if one child is the instigator and the other is innocent? For the moment, instead of focusing on the specific details of the sibling fight, we'd like you to consider the matter from a distance. The long-range goal should not be to discover who did what, but to teach your children two important lessons. First, that there won't always be someone there to "fix" the arguments, and second, that they are capable people who can manage many of their disagreements on their own.

So, try to put your concerns aside and begin to replace your role of judge with a process that treats your kids as a team. The following five approaches will help you steer clear of taking sides while you gradually encourage independence and self-reliance in your children's relationships.

1. Guide Them with Guidelines

If you're like most parents, you can't and shouldn't just with-draw from sibling fights altogether. Children do need some reasonable guidance, especially when they are young. With this in mind, let's see how Mrs. V could have handled her budding young architects differently. Rather than get caught up in end-less preaching that does not get heard, she could have set up a guideline that would solve the problem. For example, she could have used a timer, giving each child fifteen minutes to play with the Legos.

This is surely not a novel idea, but rather than focus on the idea we want to focus on how she could have implemented it without comments like "Johnny, you can't have Legos until your brother's time is up" and "Alex, don't tempt or tease him."

Mrs. V could have presented this idea in a way that would have kept her from sliding into her familiar role as judge. Instead of trying to divide and conquer, she could have used this simple skill:

* *Unite and Direct the Team*

"You two *can take turns.*"

Then she could have implemented her guideline in a way that would have kept her out of the role of a fact-finding judge by using a skill we've already mentioned:

* *Spotlight Your Own Action*

"I'll set the timer for fifteen minutes."
(Notice the timer—not Mom—will tell the kids whose turn it is.)

These simple statements connect the children and coach them to work together. Instead of making you the buffer between the kids, or allying you with one child at the expense of the other, such statements ally the children with each other and give them the opportunity to cooperate. You are not insisting that the kids shouldn't have started the fight. In fact, you are acknowledging that they have a legitimate problem. You simply refuse to take sides.

The guideline, in this case setting a timer, not only settles the dispute but gives the children ideas they can use when they begin their own negotiating. This approach offers a good compromise for younger children. If, as in Mrs. V's case, the timer

doesn't work because each of them wants to be first, you can take away the toy until the children are able to cooperate. The critical point is that in either case you are implementing a guideline that *both* children have to follow, and you are stating it without pointing a finger at either child.

2. Set Up Peace Talks

Another way to intervene and still treat 'em as a team is to set up peace talks. Peace talks are necessary when you believe a fight should be settled and your kids are not doing the settling on their own. That's when you want to enter the scene, but, rather than settle it yourself, you can expect your children to do some of the negotiating.

Some kids, though, are less than cooperative, as was the case with one of our clients, Mrs. D. She had been working hard to change the way she handled her sons' frequent fights. Just when she thought she was home free, her boys set up a rather challenging dilemma, but she definitely surprised them with a unique idea.

Mrs. D's two sons had not spoken to each other for three days because the younger one had taken his older brother's water balloons. Mrs. D initially wanted to stay out of the fight and let the boys work it out. They were not interested. So right after dinner she cornered her boys at the kitchen table and declared,

> "You two *need to sit down at the table and settle this fight.*"
> *[unite and direct the team]*

She followed with the statement,

"I'm going to sit here with you until it is settled." [spotlight your own action]

She absolutely refused to let either boy leave until the two came up with a solution. Although she was present to "encourage" the discussion, she insisted the boys work it out for themselves, and they did. They decided that the younger brother should buy a new package of water balloons with his allowance so he could give his older brother the exact number he had "borrowed." Then he would keep the rest for himself.

Another parent, Mr. N, was moved by his desperation to come up with a unique and effective peace-talk solution to a longer-term problem. He was being driven crazy by a seeming tattling tournament that his two daughters kept going strong.

The minute he came through the door at night, he was bombarded with the bickering:

"Dad, Jennifer didn't clean her room when she was supposed to."

"Amy took my colored pencils and didn't put them back."

One day, when he knew he couldn't listen to another word, and he knew his children were just as determined to give him their daily report, Mr. N was prepared with a plan to minimize the daily battles.

He told his daughters,

"From now on, you two write down the gripes and bring them up on Sunday after breakfast, when we can all give them the attention they deserve. [unite and direct the team]

"I'm not going to discuss these matters until Sunday, when I really have the time to listen." [spotlight your own action]

It worked like a charm. By the time Sunday came around, the girls had forgotten the "just for the moment" gripes designed merely to get each sister in trouble and written down the things that really affected them directly. These were the issues that were worth discussing. Most important, it wasn't just Dad doing the problem-solving; it was all three of them. While tattling was by no means over, it was minimized quite a bit, and Dad came home to a less disruptive household.

By setting up regular peace talks to deal with his kids' gripes, Mr. N accomplished three things:

1. He sent his daughters the message, you have worthwhile ideas; your ideas are important to me.

2. He set up a process that helped his children sift through their complaints and choose what was important to them.

3. And, most important, he avoided taking sides or taking over. He helped his children learn to work out their relationship.

Here's one final example of a parent's ingenuity when setting up peace talks. Mrs. S came up with a novel idea that would hit her children where it counted, in their pocketbooks. She agreed to settle their fights but explained that for taking on the job of *referee* she thought she should be paid by each child. This mom managed to do the impossible. She got her kids to unite and agree that perhaps Mom's input was not so critical. It was amazing how quickly her three children learned that they could set up peace talks even without Mom.

3. Separate without Blame

Sometimes there's just no getting around it; you've got to step in, and step in a big way. Children need to be separated. Rather than send the alleged "bad" child to her room, a parent can separate both children by saying,

> "You two *need to go to your rooms for ten minutes so you can stop fighting.*" [unite and direct the team]

If the children share a room, send one to the kitchen and the other to the dining room. Don't get sucked into determining which kid was worse. In the vast majority of cases, each child did his fair share.

Those of you with babies or toddlers may be thinking, "What about the times sibling fights involve an older child and a baby who couldn't possibly understand?" Our advice is to *set the standard by including the baby as part of the team.* Rather than entering a fight by automatically sweeping the little one into your arms and scolding the older child, you can talk to both of them.

> *"Now* you two *have to stop this or you'll have to be separated.*" [unite and direct the team]

Your older child will certainly understand that cooperation is the name of the game, and the younger one will learn soon enough.

If push comes to shove and you do have to separate them, you can carry the baby to her room and talk to the baby the same way you would talk to the older child.

> "You two *are not getting along now, so I'm going to send you to your room for about ten minutes.*" [unite and direct the team]

It makes no difference that your little one hardly understands you; your older child does. He will see that you are not playing favorites. In addition, you will avoid the easy trap of setting parent and baby against the big, bad brother.

4. Keep It Short and Simple

Thus far, we've given you ways that you can intervene without taking on the thankless job of permanent referee. Believe it or not, there will be times when you don't have to do anything at all, times when your job, and your only job, is to stay out of it. Since your children would much rather have you involved, they will invite you into their fights with talking, complaints, detailed descriptions of the injustices done to them, and so forth. If you feel you must acknowledge your children's complaints but do not want to encourage it as a way of life, there is hope.

You can respond if you must, but when you do, use the following:

* Keep It Short and Simple

There are several words in the English language that people rarely use alone but that are perfect comments for parents who want to acknowledge their kids' minor complaints while stating loudly and clearly, "I'm staying out of it." These words include "Oh!" "Really," "Hmm," "I see." These simple little words can be real lifesavers. Here's how they work:

CHILD: Jennifer tried to push me.

PARENT: Oh. [keep it short and simple]

CHILD: I hate my brother!

PARENT: Hmmm. [keep it short and simple]

Even with the complaint,

"Look at my finger. I'm sure I need a Band-Aid because of what Amy did."

Mom can apply a Band-Aid as she acknowledges the almost invisible wound with the comment

"I see." [keep it short and simple]

Don't limit yourself to using this technique with siblings. It's a great way to avoid getting pulled into arguments between any two persons, including your spouse and your child.

CHILD: Dad is so mean, he won't let me use the tools.

MOM: Oh. [keep it short and simple]

CHILD: Mom never lets me stay out as late as my friends.

DAD: Really. [keep it short and simple]

As you can see from these examples, by being brief you're not ignoring, you're just not accepting the invitation to join in. With any luck, this stance will send the message to your children: "You two need to work it out."

5. Relocate, Relocate

The ultimate way to avoid getting into your kids' fights is simply to pick up and move to another location. A perfect time to relocate is when you hear "petty" bickering begin. Comments like "My rock collection is better than yours." "You've got three more M & M's than I do." "You're breathing on me." They're your cues to get out of hearing range. Relocating will prevent you from acting on that urge to get involved, will get you away from the noise, and keep you in relative peace. If your kids are used to your involvement, you may have to find a nice, quiet hiding place in your home so they can't sniff you out so easily.

One mother, Mrs. P, thought she'd found the perfect retreat in the bathtub. Whenever she heard the beginning of a squabble that was soon to be followed by *"M-o-m,"* she would quietly high-tail it to her secret place. Unfortunately, the jig was up when her kids caught her sitting in the tub fully clothed reading her book.

Some parents just aren't fast enough to relocate; their kids run right after them, sticking like glue. If this is the case in your house or if it's too inconvenient for you to move yourself for whatever reason, you can relocate your children. But make sure you do so in a way that treats them as a team.

"You two need to finish your squabble in the basement or outside." [unite and direct the team]

If you'd like, reinforce the message by saying,

"I'm trying to read, and there's too much noise." [spotlight your own action]

This approach should confirm loudly and clearly that you are busy doing your own thing and have no intention of being drawn into the fight.

When you

- guide them with guidelines
- set up peace talks
- separate without blame

- keep it short and simple
- relocate, relocate

you are gradually teaching your kids self-reliance and coopera-tion. This ability to manage conflicts gives children the skills and confidence they need not only at home with their siblings but with peers and in other relationships that they encounter.

These lessons are important in every family, but they are especially important in families that find themselves with a perpetually innocent "good" child and an ever-provocative "bad" child. The last thing you as a parent want to do is support these roles, but that *is* what you do when you constantly inter-vene and punish the bad child or rescue the good one. You do the innocent child no favor by teaching him that he needs to depend on others to rescue him—just as you do no favor to the provocative one by responding to and reinforcing her behavior.

The benefit of treating your kids as a team can also be seen as you avoid typecasting them in any number of other confin-ing roles: the responsible older child, the pampered baby, the bully, the quiet child who has adults speak for him, and so forth. It's easy to slip unknowingly into the routine of always expect-ing the big brother to give in, always placating the screaming baby, always rescuing the "innocent" little girl, always speaking up for the shy little boy. And it's not only parents who slip into these habits; the children do too. They become accustomed to their roles and play them out, not just within the family but in other relationships as well. By treating your kids as a team, you help them avoid limiting themselves to any of these confining roles as you give them the skills and confidence they need to develop healthy, balanced relationships as they move through life.

POINTS TO REMEMBER

1. Trying to get the facts and playing judge during sibling fights can promote competition between siblings rather than cooperation.

2. Remember your long-range goal and you can avoid typecasting your child in a confining role.

3. Use the following methods to effectively handle sibling fights:

> * *Guide them with guidelines.*
>
> * *Set up peace talks.*
>
> * *Separate without blame.*
>
> * *Keep it short and simple.*
>
> * *Relocate, relocate.*

4. Use the following communication skills to treat your kids as a team:

> * *Unite and direct the team.*
>
> * *Spotlight your own action.*
>
> * *Keep it short and simple.*

THREE

Short-Circuit Power Struggles

So far we have focused on how to negotiate that delicate balance between providing limits with structure and encouraging independence by offering a child more responsibility. Now, do you think you're going to sail through parenting? Of course not.

It's true that you will have made inroads on decreasing power struggles by providing the structure that minimizes chaos and the opportunity for independence that minimizes your unnecessary input. However, you will still experience power struggles that can drive you to distraction. Is this entirely avoidable? No. There will be conflict in every household, as there needs to be, because some conflict is necessary and healthy. Conflict can be a good vehicle for creating new rules, developing independence, improving relationships, and problem-solving.

A lot of struggles in families, though, have no redeeming value. Often they are maddening, time-consuming confrontations that lead absolutely nowhere. The bad news is that no matter how conscientious a parent you are and no matter how reasonable your child may be, you and your child will, at some point, find yourselves in power struggles that may range from mildly annoying to nearly explosive. They are the result of every child's natural groping toward independence. The good news is that power struggles can be made less frequent and less intense by using the following four approaches:

- Diffuse, don't ignite, conflict.
- Use motion, not emotion.

- Make a correction with a connection.
- Stick with consequences.

These approaches will decrease your all-too-frequent flights into battle with your child.

Diffuse, Don't Ignite, Conflict

Sidestep unnecessary struggles with silence or with brief or humorous responses. When you avoid your own defensive maneuvers, your children will have no need for theirs.

What usually pulls parents into the battle zone are their own defensive maneuvers, such as overexplaining your point of view, justifying your feelings, or resorting to that old reliable, yelling.

Instead of relying on these methods, which often increase fighting, you can arm yourself with an approach that short-circuits the fighting, so those little arguments don't turn into major battles, and minimizes the frequency and intensity of the battles that are unavoidable.

When our children were very young, the simplest way we avoided a battle or tantrum was by redirecting their attention, getting them involved in something else. We've all done this, and felt relief when the potential struggle was avoided. All too soon, however, redirecting becomes a thing of the past. Our children have grown up and wised up, and it just doesn't work anymore.

So now we take the next logical step: We try to appeal to

their reason and logic. On occasion, reason does prevail, and the power struggles are avoided. All too often, however, our children's logic and our own are less than compatible. That's when potential arguments can ignite, and that's when you can turn to the following six approaches to diffuse, rather than ignite, the conflict.

1. Silence Is Golden

The first thing that will help you minimize child-to-parent disagreements is to remember to hold on to the first line of defense, "Silence is golden."

As parents, we have a hard time with this notion. We believe that when a child makes a statement, he is implicitly asking for a response. And, of course, we oblige, thinking that communication with our child is important. But here's a new notion for you: You don't have to respond to *every* comment that comes out of your child's mouth. Sometimes the most effective form of communication is keeping silent. *There are times when it's okay for your child to have the first, the last, and the only word.*

This is especially true for those times kids come up with "announcements" that sound remarkably like complaints, perhaps even remarks that unfairly blame you. Typically parents respond to these comments by suggesting, clarifying, or simply disagreeing. But these seemingly innocent comebacks have the potential to ignite a power struggle since they unwittingly challenge the kids to make their own point even more strongly. Here are two examples of how this can happen:

CHILD: These crayons lost their point after I used them just once. I hate them. I'm not using them *ever* again.

PARENT: But I just bought those crayons for you. Don't push down so hard on them. The points will last longer.

CHILD: I don't press down hard; it's these crayons. They're terrible. Why did you buy them?

CHILD: That substitute teacher was so unfair! I can't believe she wouldn't let us go outside for recess!

PARENT: You should try to understand her point of view. It was freezing outside. I wouldn't want to stand outside and freeze for thirty minutes.

CHILD: Well, our regular teacher does it. Why do we have to give up our fun?

Before you know it, you're defending your well-meaning input, and your child is defending her position. Instead of chiming in, simply listen. Show you're paying attention, but don't feel compelled to comment when it's not necessary. Remember, silence is often a valuable communication skill. It not only avoids needless defensive fencing with your child, but it also sends a powerful message:

"You have a right to complain, and I'm willing to listen without passing judgment."

Your silence is your way to acknowledge your child's problem without becoming part of it. You are not being hostile or rejecting; at the same time, you're not setting yourself up to be the fall guy for your child's anger. Believe it or not, most of the time kids say things to get them off their chests and they really don't expect you to do anything.

2. Keep It Short and Simple

Now, for those of you who feel you just *have* to say something to acknowledge your child, and for those of you who have trained your child to expect a response to every comment, make use of the same approach and skills you used in Treat 'Em as a Team. Be brief as you use those keep-it-short-and-simple skills. You remember, those easy-to-forget, undervalued words like "Oh," "Hmm," "I see," "Really"—those short lifesavers that keep you out of a fight. Let's look at two examples:

CHILD: Mom, I'm mad. There are no more cookies in the cookie jar. I never get as much as other people in this family.

PARENT: Hmmm. [keep it short and simple]

CHILD: You never pick me up at school. I hate having to take the school bus home.

PARENT: Oh. [keep it short and simple]

These overlooked words are just as versatile as they are short. You can use them in many ways. The secret is in your tone of voice and how you punctuate your line. You may want to punctuate it with a heavy period, meaning "That is the end of this discussion"; an exclamation mark, meaning "Your comment has made an impression on me"; or even a question mark, meaning "I really do want more information."

When you use the Silence Is Golden and Keep It Short and Simple skills you can:

- stop a battle before it begins
- acknowledge to your child that you've heard him
- keep yourself from becoming defensive
- avoid getting caught up in an issue that you have no intention of solving

3. Say Yes First

We've just given you two easy ways to short-circuit potential struggles by essentially ending an argument before it begins. However, there will be many times when you will want to become involved with a child's complaints or needs, times when you will need to come up with an answer or make a point, a point that your child may not want to hear. When you've got to be the bearer of bad news, you can do it in a way that reduces the chance for a struggle and may even let you come out of the discussion looking good. This is possible if you say yes first.

It's amazing how often parents use the word "no" in the course of a day.

CHILD: Can you drive me over to Sam's house?

PARENT: No, I don't want to drive in this downpour.

CHILD: Can I have a cookie?

PARENT: No, it's too close to dinnertime.

CHILD: Can I have some money?

PARENT: No, you've got an allowance.

It doesn't matter that you've followed up that no with a reasonable explanation, because your child is too busy arguing. "No" is all she heard. She's using all her energy to turn that no into a yes. We would never suggest that you give in to your child to avoid her wrath, but we do suggest that you be the one to turn that no into a yes and still make your point.

* Say Yes First

Instead of starting a sentence with that provocative word

"no," start a sentence with a word that gives you a chance to be heard—"yes." Then follow up your yes by making your point in a positive way.

- Rather than explain why your son can't go to Sam's, tell him when he *can* go.
- Rather than explain why he can't have a cookie, tell him when he *can*.
- Rather than explain why she can't have any money, tell her when she *will* get some.

Here is what we mean:

CHILD: Can you drive me over to Sam's house?

PARENT: *Yes,* as soon as it stops raining. [say yes first]

CHILD: Can I have a cookie?

PARENT: *Yes,* as soon as we're done with dinner. [say yes first]

CHILD: Can I have some money?

PARENT: *Yes,* you'll be getting your allowance in three more days. [say yes first]

Your child will be much more attentive and much less likely to escalate your passing comment into a defensive battle when you approach her with a yes instead of a no.

4. Agree, Don't Argue

Sometimes saying yes is just not enough. You may be dealing

with a more complex, emotionally charged issue that requires more than a simple statement from you. You may have to give the child some bad news and then try to soothe hurt or upset feelings. In those cases you have to be careful that your attempts to help or soothe don't result in misunderstanding and conflict you never anticipated.

Here's the story of one father, Mr. L, who had to cancel his daughter's birthday party. Before he knew what hit him, he found himself heading toward the battle zone when he was really just trying to fix her disappointed feelings.

Like all children, Tiffany had been counting the days until her birthday party. She was psyched, and Dad was rather proud of himself for pulling it together. Wouldn't you know it? There was a major snowstorm the day of the party, and it had to be canceled. Mr. L really felt for his daughter, and himself too for that matter. In his effort to help Tiffany through the disappointment, he tried to find the bright side—and that was no easy task. Instead of soothing Tiffany, he unknowingly set himself up for a struggle. Here's how:

TIFFANY: Dad, look at all the snow that's coming down.

MR. L: I see it, and I'm afraid we'll have to cancel the party today. No one can make it because of the snow.

TIFFANY: Why? I want the party.

MR. L: If you had it today it wouldn't be fun—we'll have it next week and it will be much better. We'll do something extra special.

TIFFANY: I don't want something extra special. I want my party today.

MR. L: We just can't. It's impossible.

TIFFANY: It's not impossible. You're making it impossible because you're canceling it.

MR. L: I can't control the weather.

TIFFANY: I never said you could.

At this point Mr. L was beginning to feel less and less sympathetic—he was also feeling confused about how he got into an argument and a little guilty about not finding a way to pacify his daughter. But Tiffany was doing a great job of moving him from guilt to anger. How is it that with little or no warning this well-meaning dad was magically moved to the opposing side when his intention was to show his daughter he was on her side? He was trying to take a legitimately miserable situation and make it better.

*   *   *

Sometimes your kid isn't expecting you to make it better—he just wants you to agree. When you feel this kind of an argument coming on, it's your cue to stop trying to problem-solve.

If your child is used to hearing you reason, suggest, and otherwise intervene, you won't believe the surprised look on his face when you begin to join him and complain together.

Here's what might have happened if Mr. L had used the skill:

* *Agree, Don't Argue*

TIFFANY: Dad, look at all the snow that's coming down.

MR. L: *It sure is.* I can't believe this horrible weather had to come on your birthday. I'm so aggravated; I had everything planned out perfectly for today, and now it's just not going to work. The party will have to be postponed. [agree, don't argue]

TIFFANY: What do you mean, postponed! I can't believe it! It's so unfair!

MR. L: *That's just what I was thinking.* It's so unfair. [agree, don't argue]

TIFFANY: I'm so mad! All week I was waiting for today.

MR. L: *I know what you mean.* All week I've been trying to get everything ready. I can't believe this happened, and now we will have to wait until next week. [agree, don't argue]

TIFFANY: That stinks.

MR. L: *You're so right.* [agree, don't argue]

As you can see, rather than arguing Mr. L is complaining with his daughter. As shown in this example, the trick is to start your statement with phrases that let you agree rather than argue:

"It sure is."

"That's just what I was thinking."

"I know what you mean."

"You're so right."

Then follow up by showing the same frustration or disappointment your kid is probably feeling. *By voicing your own frustration, you can commiserate with rather than try to convince your child. You may even literally take over the child's role* and state the injustice of a situation better than she does.

In addition to sidestepping an argument, this skill teaches your child a very important lesson: she doesn't have to look for someone to blame when things go wrong. Sometimes miserable situations just occur, and *rather than vent her anger against someone, she can vent that anger along with someone.* This is a hard lesson not just for children but for adults as well.

Agree, Don't Argue is not limited to situations when you wish you could solve a problem for your child. You can also use it to show that you understand your child's point of view even if you are not willing to provide a "quick fix." Here's an example of what we mean.

Frugal Patty was complaining that she didn't like spending her allowance for extras like candy and movies with her friends. She wished Mom would give her some extra money for these things even though they were what her allowance was meant for. When she complained, her mom could easily have said, "Absolutely not. You know you can't expect to get an allowance and not pay for anything."

However, this mom, quite to her own surprise, spontaneously answered:

"I know what you mean. *I hate to spend my money on little stuff, too.*"

Mrs. K was able to understand her daughter's dilemma without feeling obligated to offer a solution or being willing to solve the problem.

When we asked this mother why she was able to respond this way instead of with her usual admitted preaching, she said that she did not feel personally attacked by Patty's comment. She did not hear it to mean "You're to blame for my problem—

fix it." She did not hear it as a demand; she merely heard it as a comment.

As in this example, the ability to avoid personalizing a child's complaint is the key. When you refuse to see your child's complaints as accusations—pointing to you as the villain—you are naturally less likely to defend your position in a way that will escalate into a struggle. You can avoid the blaming and defending and instead commiserate in a way that keeps the tension to a minimum.

5. Say You're Sorry

Not all power struggles begin with the child, however. Though we hate to admit it, there are times when we reasonable adults are the instigators of troubles. Sometimes we're in a hurry, we're preoccupied, or we're exceptionally tired or cranky. We snap at our kids when they haven't done anything terribly wrong, or we respond to them with sneering or sarcastic comments. As kids mature they become rather adept at figuring out when their timing is wrong and run the other way, rolling their eyes in disgust. However, younger children don't catch on so quickly. They may pursue us despite our unfriendly mood. They may decide now is a good time for a little chat, asking a series of simple questions that result in us really blowing up and, of course, feeling quite guilty afterward.

Don't be too hard on yourself when this happens to you. The situation can actually be salvaged as a learning opportunity for both of you. You can diffuse the tension with a simple apology. Not only is your apology very reassuring, it also offers an excellent lesson for your kid. You're showing her that you can accept making a mistake. You're demonstrating your ability to look at your own behavior, take responsibility for it, and say "I'm sorry" when it is appropriate.

You'll realize how valuable this lesson is the first time your child gripes mercilessly at you and then follows it up with "I didn't mean to yell. I'm just tired and upset about what happened at school today." Now it's your child who is beginning to learn to diffuse power struggles—a lesson you'll both enjoy.

6. Use Humor

Thus far, we've taken a simple, straightforward approach to diffusing potential power struggles. But who says parents always have to stay on the straight and narrow path? Sometimes throwing a curveball can be your best bet, and that curveball is humor.

Humor is a wonderful diffuser. So many times we lose our ability to laugh when we are dealing with our children. We take parenting too seriously and forget to see the lighter side of things, and so do our kids. Kids and parents often forget that parents can be the ones who do the unpredictable.

Parents don't always have to play the straight man to their kids. It's fun to let the child be the straight man as he watches, thinking, "What will she do next?" The bottom line is, it's very hard for people to get into a fight when they're busy laughing. Humor helps us maintain an ability to laugh at ourselves—an important survival skill—and it's also a wonderful way to change the balance in the household.

Here are two examples of parents who used their creativity and made their points with humor.

Mrs. W, a family therapist, had a ritual of getting up early every morning so she could have one peaceful cup of coffee by herself. It was a well-known fact that no one bugged Mom before she had her first cup of coffee. On this particular morning, Mrs. W was in her usual place in her usual morning attire

(her old terry-cloth robe), trying to drink her morning coffee in peace. This was impossible because her daughter Rachel wanted her mother's attention *now!*

Rachel let her mom know it in no uncertain terms, as she kept issuing commands that could easily have been handled a few minutes later. Mrs. W could feel herself getting annoyed. Instead of allowing her anger to get the best of her, she trotted over to the coatrack, pulled out her furry earmuffs, placed them over her ears, and returned to her coffee.

Mrs. W hadn't uttered a word. And Commando Rachel had to take a break from her orders to laugh at Mom, who must have looked rather funny. Mom was smiling too as she finished her coffee in peace.

Another mom, Mrs. L, was angry not just at her own daughter but at her daughter's friend as well. She was on the brink of delivering a lecture laced with some yelling when she gained the presence of mind to make her statement just as loudly with humor.

Mrs. L's daughter, Beth, was having her friend sleep over Friday night. Mrs. L said to her, "I don't want you staying up all hours talking, because you have an early-morning Saturday dance rehearsal. On the other hand, I sure don't want to have to be a witch and nag you to go to bed." So they negotiated an agreement. Beth could have her friend sleep over, with lights out at 10:30. Everyone was happy.

Then Friday night came. It was way past 10:30, and Mrs. L heard plenty of noise coming from Beth's room—music, giggles, talking—and the lights were ablaze. She went in once. She went in twice. By the third time, she'd had it. She could feel herself becoming that witch! So rather than fight it, Mrs. L dressed in an old Halloween witch's costume complete with hat, a black shawl, and the kitchen broom. She "flew" in, turned off the light, took the radio, and cackled her way out. The girls burst out laughing; the lights stayed off. The message was received.

These two examples demonstrate how parents can step back for a moment and come up with funny, creative ways to avoid a fight while they stick to their guns. Now it's true, there are plenty of times when you're not feeling particularly light-hearted about an issue. If you don't feel funny, don't fake it. Insincere attempts at humor often come across as sarcasm, which can be quite hurtful. However, for those moments when you can see the lighter side, summon up the comedian in you. Loosen up; be a little unpredictable, and let that mischievous, imaginative part of you add a little spice to your parenting.

As you diminish your defensive maneuvers and increase your diffusing maneuvers, you should notice a rather immediate decrease in those annoying fights that spring up during the day. You should also notice that your child will pick up on your approach and begin to stop using defensive comments too.

POINTS TO REMEMBER

1. A child's complaint or comment does not have to be your cue to get involved in a verbal dialogue. Your silence or brief responses are good ways to keep your own defensive maneuvers in check and avoid confrontation.

2. Look for the opportunity to agree with some part of what your child says instead of just opposing him entirely.

3. If you can find some humor in a situation use it, but avoid sarcasm. You want to laugh with your child, not at him.

4. Use the following methods and communication skills to diffuse unnecessary conflict:

> * *Silence is golden.*
>
> * *Keep it short and simple.*
>
> * *Say yes first.*
>
> * *Agree, don't argue.*
>
> * *Say you're sorry.*
>
> * *Use humor.*

Use Motion, Not Emotion

When your anger is at its peak, instead of highlighting emotions with words, make your point with action. You can walk with your legs, point with your finger, or even use pantomime as you move away from the power struggle.

Now let's move to the next level of power struggles, when the arguments take on a momentum of their own. What happens when you've crossed the line of reason, when you and your child can no longer diffuse the fight? That's when parents and children end up screaming, threatening, or crying as arguments escalate into losing battles for everyone.

One parent, Mrs. C, related a scene between her son and herself that vividly demonstrates the escalation into a power struggle. She started off as a rather reasonable person and, before she knew it, ended up behaving like a raving lunatic. What moved her into the land of lunacy? Her usually sweet son, Greg!

It started off rather innocently, as Greg eyed a small glass elephant that Grandma had just given to the family. When Greg mentioned that he wanted to take it to school, his parents made it quite clear that it was to stay home. This was not an arbitrary decision. It was based on the fact that there had been two recent school "casualties"—a model airplane that Greg and his dad had painstakingly built and a large seashell.

Of course, Tuesday morning Greg began grumbling, moping, and otherwise expressing his misery about having nothing good to take to school. Dad was fortunate enough to have left for work, so Mom was left "holding the bag." After five minutes of patient sympathizing and explaining, she could see the writing on the wall; her attempts to reason were going nowhere. Her last attempt at improving the situation seemed only to add fuel to the fire. Trying to be nice, she suggested two possible substitutes.

MRS. C: Here. Why not take the globe or this really neat rock we use as a paperweight?

Greg's mumbling grew into screaming, and Mom could feel herself getting ready to explode.

GREG: Those things are dumb. (He pushed them and his mom away.) You never let me do anything I want.

MRS. C: That's not true. We'd already discussed that you couldn't take the glass elephant to school. It's too fragile.

GREG: Then I won't take anything.

MRS. C: Fine. Don't take anything. Just hurry up. You'll be late for school.

Mrs. C was upset at Greg's unreasonable attitude, but what really sent her into orbit was when she saw Greg sitting on the floor in the den with a defiant look on his face, shoes off, playing with a ball.

MRS. C: Get up and get ready now. Move it!

GREG: Idiot! (He mumbled just loud enough for his mom to hear.)

That was it! Mrs. C was beside herself. She stood over Greg screaming about his attitude. "Who do you think you are, talking that way to me?" threatening him with various punishments, "You're going to be grounded for that!" and shoving his shoes on his uncooperative feet. She lectured him from the time they got in the car until they arrived at school. "Why do we have to go through the mornings like this? With all the things I do for you, you'd think I could get a little cooperation. I have had it with you. This better not happen again. Do you understand me?" Greg said nothing when he exited the car, giving the door one hard slam.

This little scene is called a power struggle. What is it that sends an otherwise reasonable adult into orbit? Power, or the loss of it.

Parents lock horns with their children most often when they feel powerless to control their children's feelings, subdue tantrums, make their children see reason, or simply stop their children from talking back or whining. A natural response to feeling powerless is to try to gain control, and that's just what we parents do. We try to control our children, and they respond by trying to render us powerless. They flex their muscles and "show us who's really the boss." Reason and problem-solving are replaced by this vying for control. That very transition from reason to control is at the heart of power struggles. Ultimately, *everyone loses sight of the issue at hand and becomes absorbed in the issue of control.*

In the example of Greg and his mother, the issue of the glass elephant was quickly lost and just as quickly replaced with who can be the toughest. As you have probably learned through your own experience, once a struggle has reached this point, there is little you can do to turn the situation around. This is not the time to try to negotiate, understand, or even teach. Your child is not in the frame of mind to listen to you, and you're not in the frame of mind to be understanding. Instead, this is the time you want to get out of the battle as fast as possible without regretting what you say or do. You want to use motion rather than emotion.

Let's look back at Mrs. C and see what she could have done differently. She did start off rather reasonably—as any parent might—trying to explain why the glass elephant could not go to school. One cannot fault her for trying to apply reason to the situation. However, once it became clear that reason was not on Greg's mind, there was no need to continue the discussion. By staying around and talking, Mrs. C was just asking for trouble. Instead, if Greg already had the elephant, she could have gently taken it and put it away as she left the scene, finding something else to do as soon as possible. Rather than continue with well-meaning explanations that would result in yelling, screaming, and lecturing, she could have moved her body to another part of the house. She might have used those keep-it-short-and-simple words like "Oh," "Really," and "Hmm" as her feet moved quickly toward the door.

When any parent stays and talks or even screams about an issue, it implies that she might give in; it implies that if the child comes up with the right reason or just wears down the parent, she'll change her mind. So remember, if the issue is non-negotiable, don't get caught in endless verbal dialogue. Does this mean your kid will follow your lead or stop arguing? Maybe not. But if you refuse to join in the fight, you have a better chance of minimizing the length and intensity of an argument.

Let's say Greg still dawdled defiantly, shoes off, frown on, mumbling a few disrespectful words. It would have been ideal if Mrs. C could have moved away and stayed away. Besides avoiding a battle, leaving sends the message "I won't allow myself to be spoken to in a disrespectful way." Unfortunately, Mom could not stay away; she had to drive Greg to school. Five minutes before they were ready to leave, she could have visited Greg and pointed to the clock. If Greg still did not get the message, she could have escorted him and his shoes to the car as she bit her lip to avoid letting him have it.

If she'd felt she had to say something to express herself, that would have been okay. She had the right to be true to herself. But rather than screaming, she could have done it with the following:

✳ State Your Thoughts or Feelings

"I'm really angry right now. I'm too angry to talk. I need some time to think."

Parents need to tell their children how they're feeling even when they're angry. The trick is to know when to stop. When parents are angry, they have a tendency to go on and on,

becoming more angry when children do their best to show that they aren't listening. When you state your thoughts or feelings, do it honestly but briefly.

Here are three more examples of ways you can state your thoughts or feelings:

> *"My feelings are really hurt right now, and I just want to be by myself for a minute."*
>
> *"I refuse to let myself be talked to that way, so I'm taking a walk."*
>
> *"I don't want to talk now because I'm afraid I'll say something I'll regret."*

While it is important to let your kid know how you feel, it's also important to avoid exploding by substituting motion for emotion. Mrs. C could have replaced her fighting words by:

- putting the glass elephant away
- pointing to the clock
- escorting Greg and his shoes to the car without talking

There are many ways you can use motion rather than emotion. While the most obvious is just to walk away, you have plenty of opportunities to replace your emotions with motion. In fact, we've already given you a number of examples throughout the book. When parents change the environment, as with the big box, the clothes bureau, or the food snack drawer, they are using motion. When parents revert to humor or act out their feelings, as in the earmuff and witch stories, they are using motion, not emotion.

You can even resort to pantomime to avoid a burst of emotional yelling and screaming. When you want to tell your child to hurry up, you can open the garage door five minutes before it's time to go. When you want to send your child to her room, you can simply point. There are many creative ways you can use this concept. The aim is to minimize the use of words as weapons in the heat of anger and thus minimize the chance for a full-blown battle.

While walking away or resorting to pantomime may seem like a rather simple solution, it is extremely hard to do. When we get caught in an all-out power struggle, we feel our children must be taught a lesson. In fact, this may be true, but the heat of the moment isn't the time to do it.

Children rarely learn anything lasting in the midst of a power struggle. Rather than teach, *your goal is to survive and get out as soon as possible with as few casualties as possible. Save your energy for where it really counts, when you and your child are not in the throes of a power struggle.*

POINTS TO REMEMBER

1. Know you're in a power struggle when the issue at hand is lost and you find yourself fighting to control.

2. Once the issue becomes power and control, speak with any variety of actions rather than emotional words.

3. If you want to say something before you leave the scene, be brief and limit yourself to the communication skill.

✻ *State your thoughts or feelings.*

Make a Correction with a Connection

Make a connection between the child's misdeed and the resulting discipline. Whenever possible, let him experience the consequences of his behavior.

As parents we know there will be plenty of times when withdrawing from a struggle just is not enough, times when we want our children to learn a lesson. If you're lucky, the situation itself will teach the lesson while you remain on the sidelines. For example, if you've spent the morning arguing with your child about wearing shorts in 45-degree weather and she wears shorts anyway, you might expect her to come home with a new appreciation for long pants. She'll have learned her lesson naturally, by the weather and the feeling of cold wind on those bare legs. If your child misses too many soccer practices despite your reminders and is benched for the next two games, she has learned her lesson naturally, from the established rules of her league.

In instances like these, your job is to stand back and give your child the opportunity to learn. No matter how much you'd like to, *do not* try to help this learning along with "I told you so!" or "See what happens when you don't listen to me?" While such comments may be tempting, they merely stir up an argument and take the focus off the situation as the child becomes absorbed in defending his behavior. Remember, you want your child to learn to value appropriate behavior because it makes his life more manageable. And the best way for him to learn this is to keep the focus on the problem and away from power struggles with you.

While you need to take advantage of those natural learning opportunities when they occur, many times a situation will call for input from you; you'll need to step in and teach the lesson. But you have to be very clear about what it is you want your child to learn. If you want to teach that might makes right, then you can try to change your child by using intimidation and threats. If you want to teach your child to respect the value of responsible behavior, you have to take a different tack. You can begin by making a correction with a connection. This approach moves you away from "I told you so" and empty threats while moving your child toward assuming responsibility for his own behavior. Learning to make the transition from power struggles to problem solving can be difficult, and the angrier you are, the more difficult it can be.

One father, Mr. G, had an experience that very clearly demonstrates this point. In this instance, Mr. G was not only angry but very worried about how his son, Matthew, had put his safety in jeopardy. Mr. G knew he had to make an impression. So he did what he thought was right; he made an impression by coming up with a severe punishment. This is his story.

Matthew loved amusement park rides and to his pleasure found a great ride right in his own home—the garage door. First, he would push the button for the automatic garage door opener. Then he would run to the door and hold on tightly as the door pulled him up. What fun he had as he was gently lifted higher and higher, swinging his legs and feeling the soft breeze all around him. When his dad spotted him, he put an immediate stop to this "ride." He told Matthew that the garage door was not a toy and that what he was doing was very dangerous.

For a while Matthew seemed to remember his father's words. But within a couple of weeks he was swinging from the door again. In the midst of this misadventure, there was a loud plunk as the garage door came off the track. Mr. G was furious, and in retrospect he reported that he did react a little impulsively. But at the time all he could think about was how dangerous this "ride" was. He wanted to make sure his son was punished severely enough that he'd never, never do it again, so he came up with a punishment that he knew would get to Matthew.

"You are off the softball team the rest of the season," he screamed. "Maybe that will help you remember to listen to me!"

Mr. G was doing what many parents do—he was using the "no pain, no gain" approach. This approach is based on the belief that taking away something that really counts will make a child listen. Mr. G doled out this punishment because he was both angry at Matthew for not listening and worried that Mat-

thew would be hurt. By taking a strong, punitive stand, Mr. G hoped to get his son's attention.

What many parents may not know is that relying on an arbitrary punishment, like depriving a child of the thing she loves most, is the surest way to build resentment and leave a child feeling victimized. Often, disciplining with punishment fails to make an important point. It fails to show a child how she has contributed to her predicament and instead makes her focus on how unfair Mom and Dad are. *Instead of showing your child how you're in charge and how she is the victim of an arbitrary punishment, show her how she is in charge and how she is responsible for what happens to her.*

In Matthew's case, Mr. G could have avoided stiff punishments or overused regulars, like grounding or no TV. He could have made a stronger impact by implementing consequences.

Mr. G could have begun by giving himself a short time to think about what he wanted to do. While it is important to implement consequences very shortly after the misdeed, on some occasions a workable consequence is not immediately obvious, especially if you are feeling furious. Just getting Matthew out of the garage and away from his wrath would have been a sufficient start for Mr. G.

Now comes the part that is difficult for many parents, creating a consequence that has some clear, logical relationship with the misdeed. There is help. These two pairs of simple questions will help you identify such a consequence:

- Is there a problem that needs to be solved?
  How can my child solve it?

- Is there a lesson I want to teach my child?
  How can I teach it?

In Matthew's case there is a problem—the broken garage door—and Matthew needs to be involved in its repair. In addition, there is an important lesson that Mr. G wants to teach his son—Matthew must play safely and responsibly.

With this in mind, let's see how Mr. G could have proceeded. He could have started with this statement:

> *"I have the phone number of the people you need to call today to get the garage door fixed. We'll have to work out some way for you to help pay for it. Your misuse of the door made it fall off its track."*

If Matthew is capable, he, not Dad, should be calling about the repair. In that way, Matthew will confront the problem, and Mr. G will not be completely taking over the responsibility.

Let's break down the sample statement into the two skills that make a correction with a connection.

* State the Consequence

> *"I have the phone number of the people you need to call today to get the garage door fixed. We'll have to work out some way for you to help pay for it."*

This skill simply states the consequence in as clear and direct a way as possible. It is important to relate the consequence in a calm and nonthreatening manner. A delivery like "You'll see what it means to have to get something fixed, and you better get it done right" focuses on using consequences to overpower and humiliate. It focuses on making the child feel bad so she'll act good. Consequences should not be used as a weapon. Their purpose is to teach a child to look beyond the immediate result of her behavior to the long-range impact.

* Make the Connection

> *"Your misuse of the door made it fall off its track."*

While it may seem obvious to you, it's very important to verbally make the connection between the consequences and your child's behavior. Pointing out the logical cause-and-effect relationship between the behavior and the result helps your child see himself as responsible for what happened instead of blaming you or others. When you make this connection for your child, remember to avoid starting off with *"you* should" or *"you* better not." You want to make your point by focusing on the child's *action,* not the child.

This may take care of the garage, but it does not address the important issue of Matthew's dangerous misuse of property and irresponsible behavior. Mr. G would have been wise to add the following statements:

"For the next two weeks the garage is off limits and so are all the outside toys kept in the garage (bike, soccer ball, baseball glove)." [state the consequence]

"Hanging from the garage door is very dangerous and irresponsible, and I just can't trust you in the garage." [make the connection]

Note how this statement of a consequence is specific about the issue of time; it sets a limit of two weeks. Whenever possible, you should be time specific. This not only makes the consequences clear but assures the child that she will be given another chance, in this case, in two weeks.

By making a correction with a connection, you teach a lesson; avoid arbitrary, unrelated punishments; and rely on related consequences to make a lasting impact on your child. Setting up consequences instead of punishments is often a difficult transition to make, because the difference between the two is not always crystal clear. The critical difference is that you are exchanging power struggle for problem-solving, and this requires a slight but important shift in attitude. You must move away from a focus on power:

> *"My child should do what I say because I say so, and I know best."*

Move instead to a focus on problem-solving:

> *"I teach my child by letting him experience the consequences of his behavior while I give my support and provide safe structure."*

The following chart identifies the important differences between these two approaches:

PUNISHMENTS	CONSEQUENCES
Punishments make the parent totally responsible for solving problems.	*Consequences* let the child take some responsibility for himself in rectifying the problem.
Punishments teach the child to sneak or avoid getting caught.	*Consequences* make sure the child can't avoid the results of his own behavior.
Punishments encourage the child to struggle with the parent.	*Consequences* encourage the child to struggle with the problem.
Punishments are power oriented. The parent has the power.	*Consequences* are task oriented. The child has the opportunity to focus on the task and correct the problem. This encourages independence and self-reliance.

Let the Child Create the Consequence

In some situations parents have very clear ideas about what consequences they want to implement. At other times parents may not have a specific consequence in mind, they just know a correction is needed. Instead of arbitrarily developing a consequence in an effort to take immediate action, use this time as an opportunity to get your child involved. Let her help think up the consequence. Parents are often amazed at how fair and reasonable kids can be when given a chance. This is especially true when the consequence can be applied before any potential power struggle erupts.

Here's an example of a child who participated in creating a consequence. Elizabeth developed options for herself, and her input was both fair and creative.

Elizabeth loved her piggy bank. On a regular basis she would empty its contents and count out her savings. She'd ask for extra jobs around the house and immediately add her earnings to her "pile of money," as she called it. During the summer months, she'd drag out a chair, folding table, and wagon filled with items for a profitable lemonade stand. As the hot summer turned to cool fall, she knew no one would buy lemonade—even from such a persistent young lady. So with the assistance of a neighborhood friend, she developed another money-making scheme.

The two girls collected rocks from nearby yards and went door to door selling them. In forty-five minutes they made $13.61 just by calling on seven neighbors. What really put them over the top was the elderly couple next door, who gave the girls $10.00 for a rock. As they were gleefully splitting their profits on the kitchen floor, Elizabeth's mom peeked in and asked what they were doing. After the two girls told their story,

Mrs. J began conducting the inquisition: "How could you accept money from the neighbors for an old rock? Didn't you know this is wrong?"

Shortly thereafter, when she was out getting the paper, Mrs. J saw that nice elderly couple walk by. She remained rather quiet as they praised her sweet daughter for collecting money for . . . "Was it for a school or a charity?" They couldn't quite remember. Now it was starting to make sense. The neighbors had thought the girls were collecting for a good cause.

Mom, biting her lip, informed the girls that they absolutely could not keep the money. Elizabeth and her friend felt embarrassed and "stupid." They really had had no idea that the neighbors thought they were collecting for charity. But the girls were able to turn this embarrassment into an idea that Mom hadn't even thought of. If people thought they were collecting for a cause, why not donate the money to a cause? Mom had to admit it was a fine solution, one that not only taught a lesson but turned a mess into a good deed.

When you give your child the opportunity to come up with a consequence, it's important to keep three things in mind:

1. Do not attempt this when tempers are still fuming. You need to be feeling reasonably calm, and so does your child. Otherwise, you are just setting yourself up for more power struggles.

2. If you feel very committed to a specific consequence, this is not the time to open the door for suggestions. You are not likely to accept your child's input, and she will probably feel set up.

3. Let your child know from the beginning that you have the right to okay or nix any suggestions. This will help keep your child honest.

POINTS TO REMEMBER

1. Replace punishment with consequences to help your child see his responsibility in the issue at hand.

2. Make the consequence clear, time specific, and directly related to the "misdeed."

3. Present a consequence as just that—a consequence—not a punishment, threat, or attempt to control. Remember, your goal is to teach your child to respect consequences, not to respect power.

4. When possible, let your child participate in creating her consequences.

5. Sometimes creating a consequence is difficult. You can make it easier by focusing on the problem to be solved and the lesson to be learned.

6. Use the following communication skills to implement consequences:

> ** State the consequence.*
>
> ** Make the connection.*

Stick with Consequences

Stay consistent and teach with consequences, even when it seems easier and quicker not to.

It is our experience that once parents get the hang of teaching with consequences, there are still three obstacles that keep them from being consistent: when they are inconvenienced, when a child lies, or when a child tries to strike back with vengeful behavior. While inconvenience is probably the most frequent excuse we hear from parents, it is also the easiest obstacle to overcome. But when children escalate a power struggle by compounding the misdeed with lying or vindictive behavior, parents become so angry that consequences are forgotten and effective training goes out the window.

Naturally, there will be occasions when you get sidetracked and lose your cool, but you can minimize these times and maximize your ability to make a lasting impact on your kid by refusing to get distracted from consequences.

Don't Get Sidetracked by Inconvenience

As we've stated, the most common obstacle that diverts parents from consequences is inconvenience: those moments when you'd rather lecture to your child as you take care of the problem yourself, those moments when consequences seem to be more trouble than they're worth.

Here's a perfect example of one mother who thought she would make life easier on herself by ignoring the opportunity to teach with consequences and found herself cleaning up a mess while her kids didn't help.

It was a hot summer day, and Mrs. J let each of her kids, James and Meagan, invite one friend over, put swimsuits on, and fill up the tub with cold water. The kids enjoyed cooling off, and Mom enjoyed some uninterrupted peace. It was too good to be true. Mrs. J wandered into the bathroom and immediately felt sick. Every towel, every washcloth was in the tub with the kids—and these kids were old enough to know better. She was understandably furious, and she certainly had the right to blow off some steam, which she did.

She did not have to tell her children to leave the bathroom; they figured out rather quickly that the best place to be was away from Mom, and, quite frankly, Mom agreed. She wanted them out of her way while she wrung out the wet towels, mopped the floor, and made several trips back and forth to the clothes dryer.

It is a fact that Mom probably did the job a lot more efficiently and thoroughly than the children would have. However, she could have used this as an opportunity to teach the kids several skills and a valuable lesson to boot. The children could have learned how to wring out soggy towels, how to mop, how to use the dryer, and, above all, how to take responsibility for their own behavior. If Mrs. J felt she could not hand over all the cleanup, she could have selected some manageable portion for the kids to do.

While it may seem less convenient at the moment, sticking with consequences will make life easier for you and your child in the long run.

Don't Get Sidetracked by Lying

The second obstacle that seems to divert parents from teaching with consequences is when a child's lying compounds a problem. Parents often become so absorbed in the lying that the issue of the misdeed gets lost. Usually what results is a minimum amount of teaching and a maximum amount of yelling. The following story offers a good example of how lying can get parents off the track and prevent them from teaching a lesson and making a lasting impact with consequences.

Mr. K's son, Brad, was building a fort in his backyard with several of his friends. The boys dragged over a few logs, meant for firewood, some rocks, and anything else that looked like potential building material. Of course, to make a really good fort, they needed tools—Mr. K's tools. Brad rummaged through the toolbox, grabbing a hammer, screwdriver, and an assortment of garden tools for digging. The boys put a lot of effort into this project and were rather proud of themselves. As they were moving toward completion, it started to drizzle, and, being smart enough to come in out of the rain, they headed back home as the tools remained on their job site.

That weekend Mr. K settled into the garage, planning to finish fixing a table leg that was already an annoyance. It became even more so when he could not find the screwdriver he needed. After looking for a good twenty minutes, he gave up and took the dog out for a quick walk in the backyard. Guess what he found.

Mr. K was exasperated. This was not the first time Brad had "forgotten" to return tools he'd borrowed. Brad and his friends had had other fort-building adventures, and while Mr. K felt they were responsible enough to use some select tools, he'd told Brad in no uncertain terms that they had to be carefully put back. Mr. K wasn't going to let Brad get away with this. He went back to the house and set a trap for his son.

MR. K: Did you happen to see my tools? I've been looking all over for my flat-tip screwdriver.

BRAD: No, I didn't. Uh, I don't think so.

MR. K: Oh really? Then how did they manage to end up outside next to your fort?

BRAD: I don't know.

MR. K: You're lying to me.

BRAD: I didn't lie exactly. I just said I don't know.

MR. K: Well, that's lying. It seems I can't trust you.

Mr. K's anger is understandable. Nothing moves us to anger quite as quickly as lying. We all know that lying is completely unacceptable, just as we all know that at some point most children will lie or at least twist the truth to some degree. Naturally, we want to discourage lying, and often the best way to do that is to avoid setting up the opportunity to lie with questions like "Did you see my tools?" You can move away from setting up lies and instead approach the problem using the two pairs of questions designed to teach your child a lesson in responsibility:

- Is there a problem that needs to be solved?
  How can my child solve it?

- Is there a lesson I want to teach my child?
  How can I teach it?

In this case, rather than become absorbed in a lie, Mr. K could have held up the tools and used that old reliable skill

✳ State the Facts without Blame

"These tools were outside by the 'fort.'"

By stating the facts without blame, Mr. K could have bypassed accusations and his son's defensive maneuvers as he moved toward dealing with the task at hand. There would have been no way his son could have argued with this statement, and there would have been no need for Mr. K to justify his next as he made a correction with a connection.

"This screwdriver needs to be replaced by you [state the consequence]

"because it's rusty from the rain." [make the connection]

"For the next six weeks I'm keeping all the tools locked in the toolbox, and I won't lend them [state the consequence]

"because I need to know my tools will be returned and treated carefully." [make the connection]

The point is that you can stop using questions that set up your child by creating opportunities to lie. Whether your question is as benign as "Did you brush your teeth?" when you know he didn't or "Were you at the neighbor's house like you said you'd be?" when you know she wasn't, you would do well to stop creating opportunities for your child to lie and stay focused on teaching with consequences.

Naturally there will be occasions when a child's lie is not provoked by a question from you. Then what? You can still move beyond the lie to the issue at hand. The following story, proudly told by Mrs. S, one of our parenting group mothers, will show you how.

Andrew came home from school with his backpack filled to the brim as usual. What was not usual was that, instead of dumping it on the kitchen floor, he took it up to his room, where it belonged. In retrospect, Mrs. S believed this should have been her first clue that something was up. Andrew never put his backpack in his room.

Unsuspecting, Mrs. S was busy getting ready for her evening job. The baby-sitter arrived, and Mrs. S went into Andrew's room to say good-bye. There was Andrew, playing with a telescope that looked remarkably like the ones she had seen at his school. In fact, it still had the masking-tape label that read MRS. KATZ'S SECOND-GRADE ROOM. When Andrew saw Mom, he quickly tried to hide the telescope behind his back. This only inspired his mother's curiosity and made her quite sure Andrew had taken it without asking.

Then Andrew put his foot directly into his mouth. "I found this outside, and I thought it might belong to someone, so I took it home for safekeeping. I bet it's Michael's. He has one just like it. It probably fell out of his backpack on his way home."

Mom decided to intervene so Andrew would not dig an even deeper hole for himself.

"I see that the telescope has Mrs. Katz's name and room number on it. [state the facts without blame]

"The school needs to be called now so someone knows where the telescope is, and the telescope has to be returned to your classroom tomorrow [state the consequence]

"since it seems to have been taken without permission." [make the connection]

Many times you will want to, and should, address the fact that your child lied, and you can do so directly by firmly stating, "Lying is not acceptable." Then you can move on and invest your energy in creating a consequence appropriate to the situation. By refusing to set your child up to lie, by refusing to give undue attention to lying, by refusing to be sidetracked from dealing with a misdeed by becoming absorbed in a lie, you will truly decrease the occasions for lying and can stick with teaching through consequences.

Don't Get Sidetracked by Revenge

A third occasion in which parents tend to overlook consequences is when the child (or parent) has moved beyond a power struggle to a struggle for revenge. These are situations when children up the power struggle and not only want to show their parents who is boss but also want to hurt them.

Children can move to revenge in a variety of ways: They can purposely damage something belonging to their parents, embarrass their parents, refuse to be affected by anything their parents say, and so forth. While these kinds of scenarios can and will occur with most children at some time, they occur with remarkable frequency in homes where the need to be right, the need to be boss, and the need to win permeate many aspects of the parent-child relationship. They occur when parents un-knowingly get swept up in the vindictive behavior, and both parents and children end up feeling hurt. Often the only way a child knows to convey the depths of his own hurt is to hurt back, so the cycle of vindictive behavior begins.

That was exactly the case with Mrs. D and her daughter, Katie. Mrs. D was never certain how the fights started, but all too often she and Katie were at odds.

Mrs. D recounted one day in particular when Katie was acting impossible. Mrs. D truly forgot what started the shouting match, but she did remember that it ended with her taking Katie to her room and telling her not to come out until she gave her permission. That was supposed to be the end, but it wasn't. Katie started taking toys out of her room and throwing them downstairs. If Mom thought she was going to overpower Katie, she had another thought coming.

They were in the throes of an all-out power struggle. Mrs. D told Katie to "pick those toys up immediately."

"No," responded Katie, as she threw one more toy down the steps.

"If you don't pick those toys up now, I'm giving them away!"

Now do you think Katie scurried down the stairs, picked up her toys, and retreated to her room? No way! Instead, she yelled out, "I don't care what you do!" And just to make sure her mom got the point, she darted into her mother's room, grabbed a dress off the bed, crumpled it up, and threw it right at her mother. "So there!" she said as she retreated to her room. Katie had now moved this skirmish from a struggle for power to a vengeful attempt to affect Mom by hurting her.

There isn't a parent who would not want to follow that child upstairs and do something to get back at her. When parents feel hurt or pushed to the limit, it's very hard for them to pull out of the fight, because they believe that doing so is backing down and giving in to their children. They believe that they must demonstrate their own toughness and respond by matching their kids' vindictive behavior and showing how powerful they can be.

In fact, withdrawing from the fight not only keeps you from losing your cool but conveys two important points. First, it shows your child you will not be goaded into a fight even when

your child resorts to revenge. Second, and this is very important, it shows your child that fighting and vindictive behavior will not move you toward him, even in anger. It will move you away. What should Mrs. D have done? Despite the intensity of her feelings, she should have begun by using motion, not emotion.

Mrs. D might have used motion by retrieving her dress and by taking the toys off the stairs, putting them in a box to be dealt with later. While such a reaction may seem difficult or distasteful, it will keep you from flinging out a consequence as a threat—a threat that your child will see as a dare. There's no doubt that it's very hard to withdraw and not defend yourself or strike back with some choice words of your own. But, as with all struggles or misdeeds, you want to keep yourself and your child out of the victim mode and, whenever possible, in the problem-solving mode. With Katie, a good way to have started would have been to wait for the storm to pass and then say,

> *"The toys on the stairs are put away for two weeks [state the consequence]*
>
> *"because they were not being treated properly." [make the connection]*
>
> *"Also, I'll need to use some of your birthday money to get my dress pressed [state the consequence]*
>
> *"because it got wrinkled when it was thrown down the stairs." [make the connection]*

And what if the response to all your hard work and efforts to teach is "I don't care!"?

That's the time you need to remember your own goal. All too often we base our sense of success on our children's immediate response rather than on our own ability to stick with a reasonable consequence. Often we switch our tactics in mid-stream because our children don't respond as we expect. *Parents need to learn to base their sense of the "success" of their approach on what they've done—not necessarily on how their children respond.* We have to set the pace and direction rather than follow a child's lead toward power and revenge. The goal is to teach our children to respect consequences, not power.

This does not complete the picture, however. Diminishing power struggles and implementing consequences is not enough. There is one more avenue we need to address, an avenue that is most important and most difficult when kids are acting out and making everyone's life miserable. That avenue is encouragement. Every parent knows how important good self-esteem is to every child. That's a given. But it is very hard to keep this goal in sight when parents feel they can find little positive to say, and, of course, this is the time children need to be picked up the most. With this in mind, let's turn our attention to maximizing a kid's self-esteem.

POINTS TO REMEMBER

1. Take time out for training, even when dealing with the problem yourself would be much easier.

2. Don't set your child up to lie by asking her questions. Change your focus from "who did it?" to "what can be done?" and keep yourself focused on implementing consequences.

3. Avoid following suit by moving to revenge, even though your child may be vengeful.

4. Learn to base your sense of success on what you've done, not necessarily on how your child responds.

5. Use the following communication skills as you stick with consequences:

> ** State the facts without blame.*
>
> ** State the consequence.*
>
> ** Make the connection.*

FOUR

Maximize Self-Esteem

As parents we all know how important self-esteem is to every child. Yet it is understandable that encouraging self-esteem is often the last thing on parents' minds if they are moving from one struggle to the next. What you need to remember during those frustrating moments is this: The thing that often incites the battles between you and your child is your child's low self-esteem. When children feel they can't affect their parents by cooperating, they may well try to make an impact through arguing and power plays. That's when parents retreat from esteem-building comments to criticizing and correcting comments.

self-esteem goes down ⟳ power struggles go up

This cycle leaves both parents and children feeling discouraged, inadequate, and even hopeless. Parents can break this cycle— not just by trying to short-circuit those power struggles but also by focusing on maximizing their children's self-esteem.

Naturally, you don't want to even try to muster up positive comments in the midst of an argument. That's not the appropriate time or place. But you can capitalize on other moments, when you and your child are at relative peace. You can use your energy to accent the positive for your child and for yourself.

The key to being encouraging even during difficult times is to use the following four approaches:

- Make the most of ho-hum moments.
- Tune in to your kids so they don't tune out.

- Make the evidence evident.
- See the small successes along the way.

With these approaches, you can boost the self-esteem of that less than confident child as well as that of the child who has a positively glowing self-image.

Make the Most of Ho-Hum Moments

The key to being encouraging even in the hardest of times is to realize the importance of the simple, everyday happenings that are all too often ignored.

To illustrate this point, let's take a look at Mrs. A and her son, Arnie. They seemed to be heading for the battle zone a lot more often lately.

Arnie's parents had recently brought home a new baby sister. Once was bad enough, but this was Arnie's second time around for dealing with this upsetting change in his life. Mom and Dad were "getting theirs" for doing such a traitorous deed to their firstborn son.

As the fights increased between Mom and Arnie, Mrs. A was more and more convinced that she had to find a way to turn things around. One day, after lots of encouragement and support from some parents in her group, she made up her mind. She would give Arnie the kind of attention he needed to feel reassured and good about himself. Determined not to let any opportunity pass by, she was going to arm herself with a full array of compliments that she could shower on Arnie when he came home from school. Here's how that afternoon went.

Shortly after 3:00 P.M., Mrs. A heard the familiar squeak of the back door and caught a glimpse of Arnie as he raced by her, grabbed a handful of cookies, and made a beeline for the TV.

"Arnie, I want cookies, too," his three-year-old sister clamored as she attempted to give him a big, sloppy hello. "Mommy, Arnie has cookies, and I don't." Arnie reluctantly handed her a cookie from his stack, saying, "Quiet, I can't hear the TV." He had switched the channel from his sister's "Sesame Street" (he knew she wouldn't mind) to his favorite cartoon. Just as he plopped himself down on the couch, the phone rang, and, to get some quiet, Arnie picked it up and shrieked for his mom, who was only a few feet away. Now he could finally settle back to enjoy his afternoon zone-out time as he petted the family dog.

While this was a fairly typical day, for Mrs. A it presented a real challenge. Where were those simple, natural opportunities to build self-esteem? She was waiting for Arnie to show her an art project so she could compare him to Picasso or a homework assignment so she could rave about his good work. Mrs. A was discouraged, and, in truth, she didn't see a whole lot going on that afternoon that was worth complimenting. Even more truthfully, if she hadn't been feeling so loving or wanted to be so positive, she could have seen some mildly irritating behaviors that afternoon.

"What was I supposed to say?" she asked as she reported to the group the next week.

"I really like that you hogged the cookies."

"I really like the way you switched your sister's TV show and plopped down on the couch."

"I especially appreciated how you decided to move right to the TV and bypass any possible homework assignment."

Because Mrs. A could not find anything positive or encouraging to say, she decided to say nothing at all. That was a step in the right direction. By squelching her impulse to focus on minor everyday annoyances, Mrs. A was beginning to train herself to spend more energy looking for opportunities to encourage instead of responding to passing irritations. The problem remained, though; she could not find any uplifting comment to squeeze out.

Mrs. A needed to learn the skills that would help her find something positive even when the pickings were slim. Here's how she—or you—could have literally pulled encouragement out of a hat. She could start by returning to the most basic skill for pointing out the positive:

✳ *Enjoy Who Your Child Is*

"It's sure good to see you. You really brighten my day," as she puts her arm around her son's shoulder.

The first step in maximizing ho-hum moments is to stop waiting for your child to produce something praiseworthy, act discouraged, or specifically request some encouragement with leading questions like "Did you see my great throw?" or "Do you like this project?" You can start where there are no expectations for performance at all. The easiest place is with something simple. Begin to show your child that you unconditionally, indisputably enjoy who she is. There is nothing for the child to live up to—no expectations and no performance standards. Many parents give this unconditional encouragement quite naturally early in the morning, before any hint of problems, or at bedtime, when they're tucking in that angelic, sweet-smelling child. Don't limit yourself. Be creative, and use this form of encouragement throughout the day when your child least expects it.

It's important to be honest, though. There are plenty of times you don't enjoy your child. In fact, there are times when your child is driving you crazy. These are not the times to offer encouragement. Wait for the moment you can say something positive and mean it!

Here are five statements that you can use to enjoy who your child is:

> *"It's sure good to see you."*
>
> *"I really enjoyed being with you today."*
>
> *"Hi, Tiger." (or whatever special nickname applies)*
>
> *"Hope you are having a good day." (a special note in a lunch box)*
>
> *"You sure are huggable." (while giving your child a surprise hug)*

The second way that Mrs. A could have made the most of a ho-hum moment was to have used the following skill:

✳ *Highlight an Everyday Moment*

> *"Arnie, B.J. really seems to enjoy you petting him so gently on his tummy. You sure have a way with him."*

Like Mrs. A, many parents wait for an ideal situation so they can compliment their children. Many times, that moment never arrives. Then what? We'd like to suggest an alternative. Look at an uneventful everyday moment and highlight it.

What could be more uneventful than Arnie petting the dog? Not much. Nonetheless, this easy-to-ignore occasion is a good opportunity for building self-esteem. As you can see, when you highlight everyday events, you can begin to pull encouragement out of thin air. There are plenty of seemingly uneventful times during the day when you can use this skill. Consequently, this is a valuable source for unlimited encouragement.

Let's look at three more examples of highlighting an everyday moment:

"You chose a good variety of food for lunch."

"What a perfect choice of clothes for this weather. It will keep you warm."

"Your teeth sure look clean. You are doing a good job of brushing them."

A third easy-to-overlook skill for raising self-esteem is to

✴ *Appreciate Your Child's Help*

"Thanks, Arnie, for answering the phone for me."

While it can be pretty natural for parents to show appreciation when children are helpful, this form of encouragement can often be forgotten if the help is not exactly what parents had in mind. If Mrs. A had really been on her toes, she could have said,

"Jennifer really enjoyed that cookie you gave her. Thanks for sharing with her."

Note that Mrs. A would have continued to ignore the minor irritants, forgetting the fact that Arnie kept five cookies and turned his sister's TV program off.

Now this last comment may be stretching things a bit; you may not be able to get those words out of your mouth, and if so, don't. There are a lot of other choices throughout the day. Again, it's important to be true to yourself. At the same time, don't let a good opportunity to appreciate your child go by because it's surrounded by some other behaviors that don't completely delight you.

Here are three additional examples of simple ways to appreciate your child's help:

"I really appreciate your help by putting your dirty cup in the sink."

"I wouldn't have gotten this room cleaned if you hadn't pitched in."

"Thanks for reminding me that the timer went off."

When you show your child that you appreciate her help—even under less than ideal circumstances—you let her see herself as a cooperative person. She begins to recognize and value her ability to cooperate, and she also learns to acknowledge this ability in others.

These three skills—enjoying who your child is, highlighting an everyday moment, and appreciating your child's help—can help you encourage self-esteem under any circumstances. When you accent the positive, you offer your child the best type of encouragement of all, the kind that says, "You are great just as you are."

Perhaps the most important aspect of accenting the positive for your child is that by doing so you are also identifying the positive for yourself. You are not only lifting your child's self-esteem but are also encouraging yourself as a parent. This sets the stage for a less conflictual, closer relationship—in which you and your child can understand and respect each other's feelings. You may start off feeling unnatural as you put these encouragement skills into practice. But before long you'll be seeing your child in much broader and fuller ways. You'll be teaching yourself and your child two powerful lessons: to see and believe in the many solid, positive things your kid does that were often previously ignored; and to stop focusing on mistakes and problems and start putting that effort into acknowledging the acceptable, enjoyable qualities of your child.

POINTS TO REMEMBER

1. Don't wait for something "praiseworthy" in order to give your child encouragement. Use the small, easy-to-ignore parts of the day to raise her self-esteem.

2. Learn to change your own outlook, and use your eyes and ears to find small esteem builders rather than small problems.

3. Make the most of ho-hum moments by using these three communication skills:

> * *Enjoy who your child is.*
>
> * *Highlight an everyday moment.*
>
> * *Appreciate your child's help.*

Tune In to Your Kids so They Don't Tune Out

Instead of always working so hard at making your children understand what you say, work hard at understanding and acknowledging what they say.

When we begin to pay closer attention to our children's self-esteem, we are likely to become even more sensitive to those occasions when our children are feeling discouraged. We want to do what we can to build them back up, especially when they come up with generalized statements like

"I'll never be good at sports."

"I'm not as pretty as Susie."

"I don't have any friends."

Most parents set to work trying to minimize their children's negative feelings by pointing out their positive qualities.

"Sure you're good at sports. You're good at soccer already."

"Of course you're pretty, and you're beautiful to me."

"You have friends. Last week Matt invited you over."

But many times these well-intentioned responses simply inspire a child to fight back. The harder the parent tries to point out the positive, the harder the child clings to the negative. *Instead of working so hard to make your child understand and accept what you say, you can work hard to understand and accept what your child is saying.* The following example illustrates just what we mean.

Josh was a pro at criticizing himself, and Mr. and Mrs. B spent a lot of energy trying to talk their son out of these negative feelings. But the more they tried to pick up Josh with compliments and proof that he was good, the harder Josh worked to put himself down. Mr. and Mrs. B wanted to help Josh develop more confidence in himself, but they were painfully aware that their efforts seemed to backfire. What happened one night when Mr. B was discussing Josh's math homework with him really brought this to light.

JOSH: I'll never finish these math problems.

MR. B: Of course you will.

JOSH: Why can't I be as smart as my friend Eddie? He already finished his assignment at school.

MR. B: That's not true. You *are* smart. Look at the good grades you make.

JOSH: Oh, Dad, the other kids are better than I am in this.

As you can see, these attempts to encourage and raise Josh's self-esteem were met with Josh's determination to prove his point. After this back-and-forth discussion, both Josh and his dad felt frustrated. Mr. B felt Josh was unwilling to accept his opinion, and Josh felt his father completely misunderstood him.

It just didn't make any sense to Josh's parents. Even though Josh won the battle, he walked away a loser. He felt really down on himself. They wanted to learn some other way to handle Josh's low self-esteem.

First of all, Mr. B needed to fire himself from his job of always trying to build Josh up. Instead of trying to push Josh into feeling better, he needed to slow down and listen. Mr. B could have shown his support this way:

JOSH: I'll never finish these math problems.

MR. B: You must really be feeling upset about your math homework for tomorrow.

JOSH: Why can't I be as smart as my friend Eddie?

MR. B: You're annoyed that Eddie finished his work at school and you had to bring yours home tonight.

These few words—

"You must really be feeling upset about your math homework for tomorrow."

"You're annoyed that Eddie finished his work at school and you had to bring yours home tonight."

—illustrate two important skills.

* *Identify the Feeling*

This is your way of letting your child know you understand. Many parents know this skill as "active listening," which was developed by Thomas Gordon in his book *Parent Effectiveness Training.* The idea is to repeat the child's feelings so the child feels heard.

✳ *Nail Down the Specific Event*

For this ingredient, we have added an important twist to the listening skill. You can pinpoint the specific event that is discouraging rather than simply repeat your child's feelings or go along with her generalized sense of discouragement.

Here's how Mr. B's hypothetical responses would break down:

"You must really be feeling upset [identify the feeling]

"about your math homework tomorrow." [nail down the specific event]

"You're annoyed [identify the feeling]

"that Eddie finished his work at school and you had to bring yours home tonight." [nail down the specific event]

As you can see, Mr. B doesn't have to let Josh get stuck feeling generally "stupid." He can identify Josh's feelings in relation to a particular difficulty. This is very important. So often kids like Josh develop their self-concept through generalizations. They fail to see an obstacle or disappointment as just one problem that they can't solve. They feel stupid altogether and develop an attitude that says, "I just can't do it." This kind of generalized discouragement, particularly about learning, can make school a source of trouble and anxiety. By identifying the feeling and nailing down the specific event, you can show understanding while narrowing down the problem from something overwhelming to something more manageable. Not only does this give your child a sense of being understood, but it also teaches her to put things in proper perspective so she can move on.

One important area where these skills keep parents from becoming the enemy, and let them end up as allies, is their kids' peer relationships. As children grow up, peer relationships become the most important and the most painful part of their lives. It's no wonder that parents want to run in and fix their kids' feelings whenever they can. Unfortunately, these attempts often leave parents in the dust as their inconsolable kids storm off with comments like "You just don't understand."

Here's an example of what we mean. Mrs. J tried to show her daughter, Lucy, that she was on her side and ended up starting an argument.

Lucy was fighting back the tears as she and her family walked over to the school carnival. Mrs. J knew why. It was because Lucy had invited her friend Sara to go to the carnival with her several days before. Lucy had excitedly been calling Sara during the day to discuss what they'd do, but Sara was out and never returned the calls. Finally, Lucy reached Sara's dad, who told her that Sara had gone to the carnival with Joan. Lucy felt crushed. "How could she do that? We made plans days ago. I don't have any good friends."

Her mom felt hurt for Lucy and angry—particularly since this so-called friend had done similar things to Lucy on other occasions. She hated to see Lucy hurt like this, and said, "Anyway, didn't Sara do this before? Remember just last week, she was supposed to sleep over and changed her mind at the last minute. Friends like that aren't worth it. You're too good of a friend to let yourself be treated like that."

Mrs. J said this in the most loving way—with her arm around her daughter as they walked. Unfortunately, her efforts to console Lucy only upset her more, and she ended up on the receiving end of her daughter's misery.

"We have fun together, Mom. I like being with her, and sometimes she can be a good friend. You don't really know her. You don't know my friends. How can you say that?"

Mrs. J was trying to be helpful, yet Lucy and her mom were locking horns. What made it worse was that they both felt the same way—hurt and angry about what had happened.

Let's see how Mrs. J could have shown her understanding and changed Lucy's generalized bad feelings about herself to disappointment about a specific situation.

"You are really angry at Sara [identify the feeling]

"today because she left without you." [nail down the specific event]

"You are worried [identify the feeling]

"about having a friend to be with at the carnival." [nail down the specific event]

Instead of fueling the fire and trying to blame the other girl, Mrs. J could have pinpointed Lucy's feelings and helped her redefine them. She could have moved from the generalization

"I don't have any good friends."

to the more specific, limited feeling

"You are really angry at Sara today."

Here are some additional examples that demonstrate identifying the feeling and nailing down the specific event:

Your daughter just got a new haircut, and she keeps looking at herself in the mirror and trying to "do something" with her hair. She looks disgusted and says,

"I'm not pretty."

You can say,

"I can see you're feeling upset [identify the feeling]

"about the new haircut you got this morning." [nail down the specific event]

Your daughter loves gymnastics and she wanted to be in the advanced group, but she didn't make it. She says,

"I'm not good at gymnastics."

You can say,

"You sound disappointed [identify the feeling]

"that you didn't get promoted to the next level." [nail down the specific event]

Your son just came in the house loaded down with books, and he has a Cub Scout meeting in an hour. He says,

"I hate my teacher."

You can say,

"You're really angry [identify the feeling]

"that your teacher loaded you up with homework today." [nail down the specific event]

What you are doing is gently leading your child from an overall sense of defeat without challenging his feelings or saying who was right and who was wrong. The child will learn to take your direction and begin to understand his feeling in relation to a specific, concrete situation.

This is an invaluable skill. With it, feeling good or bad becomes less mysterious, less arbitrary, and less out of control. This may not make your child feel one hundred percent better, but it will make her feelings more manageable. Once more—when you begin to listen to and understand your child—you increase the chance that she can listen to you as well.

POINTS TO REMEMBER

1. Don't rush in and fix your child's feelings every time he seems discouraged.

2. Put your emphasis on showing your child that you understand her feelings instead of pushing your own well-intentioned feelings onto her.

3. Make your child's feelings more manageable by translating a generalized feeling into a particular feeling related to a specific event.

4. Use the following communication skills to tune in to your kid:

  * *Identify the feeling.*
  * *Nail down the specific event.*

Make the Evidence Evident

Rather than focus on your child's potential, focus on his current, irrefutable accomplishments by describing what you see and remembering his past, already mastered accomplishments.

What about those times when you want to do something more to boost your child, to go beyond understanding and respecting your child's feelings? Fortunately, you've already set the stage, for even those kids who are hard to encourage become more receptive once you've shown you can recognize and understand their feelings. Now you're in a position to offer encouragement boosters that can't be refuted.

Here's how one dad, Mr. O, moved from being the object of his daughter's defeated, angry feelings to being a supportive father who was in a perfect position to raise his daughter's confidence level in spite of herself.

Heather, a perky, enthusiastic kid, usually took on new challenges successfully. That is, until she signed up for basketball and played her first game. As with many things, she expected to do great, but this time she was in for a surprise. She couldn't even handle the ball, let alone make a basket. Her parents were very tempted to point out how David, her older cousin, had improved almost immediately; they were sure she would do the same. However, after they took one look at their daughter's dejected face, they threw that idea out. Instead, her dad suggested that they practice together on the weekend.

Heather was convinced she couldn't even throw the basketball. Her dad was convinced otherwise. Every time Mr. O pointed out that Heather was doing okay, she refuted his compliments.

MR. O: You're going to be a great basketball player.

HEATHER: No, I'm not.

MR. O: Sure you are. You've got great coordination.

HEATHER: You're just saying that.

Mr. O could see he was getting nowhere fast. He pulled out some new skills he'd recently learned in our parenting group and got his daughter's attention with the statement

"You really are discouraged about your basketball playing this afternoon." [identify the feeling and nail down the specific event]

But Mr. O felt it was not enough. He wanted to give his daughter a boost she couldn't refute. He was ready to use some additional skills. As he was soon to learn, the key to offering unarguable encouragement is to stop focusing on a child's potential and instead address the child's present and past accomplishments.

Mr. O could have used two skills that are as encouraging as they are indisputable.

* *Describe an Action*

He could have replaced the comment

> *"You're going to be a great basketball player."*

with comments like

> *"You passed that ball right to me."*
>
> *"You had three dribbles in a row."*
>
> *"You caught that bounce pass the first time."*

When your child resists encouragement, you can take an approach that simply describes all the small actions you observe without adding any evaluative words. Exclamations alone—"great," "terrific," and "wow"—are natural encouragers, and many children will beam when you use them. However, if, like Heather, your child is having trouble hearing compliments, play it safe by moving to statements that only describe the action, without evaluating it.

A child might be able to argue with the comment

> *"You'll be a great player."*

But there's no way she can argue with

> *"You caught that bounce pass the first time."*

The second booster Mr. O could have used with Heather is the skill

* *"Remember When"*

> *"Remember when you learned to ride your two-wheeler? You started out falling, not being able to steer, and in a matter of days you were sailing along."*

Mr. O could have reminded Heather of a past accomplishment that she could draw on for encouragement. Children have a warehouse full of past accomplishments. Unfortunately, many children and parents minimize their significance. When parents become busy helping their children do better, they forget the importance of pointing out what their children have already done well. When your child is not satisfied with his current progress, you can use the small achievements of the past to raise his morale.

There's no guarantee that Heather will master basketball as she mastered riding a bike, but that's not the point. The real purpose of the "remember-when" skill is to continue to tap the child's inner resources by recalling past accomplishments.

A child can easily accept both of these forms of encouragement because they are honest. Most important, these comments do not place expectations on the child's future performance. *You are commenting on what is or what was—not on what could be, and that's often the best place to start.*

Let's briefly review these skills. First, how to describe an action:

Your six-year-old child comes to you discouraged because he couldn't swim the length of the pool. You might say:

> *"You swam five strokes under the water without even taking a breath."*

If you're really desperate, you might say:

> *"You cupped your hands, and your strokes really pulled you through the water."*

Or your child is showing you she is able to do a cartwheel. You might say:

> *"Your legs were perfectly straight when you landed on your feet."*

If you're really desperate, you might say:

> *"You pushed your hands off the floor, and you had a lot of power in your cartwheel."*

Or you're bravely listening to your child practice his musical instrument. As he screeches along his merry way, you might say:

"You really arched your fingers to play the low notes on the violin."

If you're really desperate, you might say:

"You really used a lot of lung power to get those high notes out of the clarinet!"

Now let's review how to use "remember when" statements:

"I remember when you felt so frustrated trying to learn last week's spelling words, and you managed to learn them in only three days."

"I remember when you thought you would never swim without your floaties, and in one summer you not only swam, you jumped off the diving board."

"Remember when you first went to kindergarten and were scared because you didn't know anyone? You made lots of friends and didn't feel frightened anymore."

By adding these two skills to your repertoire, you can begin to expand your own view of accomplishment and your confidence-building comments. But don't restrict yourself to using these forms of encouragement when your child is discouraged. They are just as effective when he is feeling good about his accomplishments. Rather than limit yourself to traditional comments—"That's a *great* paper you wrote!" or "That was a *terrific* grade on your test!" or "You were *tremendous* in the school play!"—you can use an additional form of encouragement that will teach you and your child to identify observable actions so that you can both savor the moment and recall past successes.

POINTS TO REMEMBER

1. When your child is feeling discouraged, don't overwhelm her with encouraging comments about her potential.

2. Use achievements of the past to help your child feel good about the present. Children have a warehouse full of past accomplishments and resources they can draw on for encouragement.

3. Keep in mind that you can give your child a sense of success and still keep your feedback honest.

4. Use the following communication skills to make the evidence evident:

> * *Describe an action.*
>
> * *"Remember when."*

See the Small Successes along the Way

While it's okay to praise good results, you can multiply self-esteem builders by highlighting the many small steps that occur as your child tackles each task.

Now that you have learned to pull encouragement out of a hat, show support and understanding, and give a boost your child can't refute, you're ready to focus on the four additional building blocks of self-esteem, building blocks that downplay results and play up small successes. But first we want to point out what you should *not* do. *For the fact is that what often gets in the way of improving children's self-esteem is their parents' effort to improve the children.*

Here's a telling story of how one well-meaning father, Mr. F, got so wrapped up in helping his son, Sam, improve that he ended up being discouraging rather than encouraging.

It was Sam's Little League game. He was just beginning to feel comfortable with the rest of the kids on the team and the other dads who were coaching. Sam's mom and dad were sitting on the lawn with the rest of the parents. Mr. F started off great. He was as encouraging and supportive as he could be. He cheered in all the right places and really showed an interest.

When Sam's team went into the outfield in the third inning, Sam was put on third base, and he was delighted. Until then, Sam had been so far out in the outfield he hardly knew what was going on. Dad, a lefty like Sam, was not so delighted. "He's a lefty. You never play a lefty at third, because his reach for the ball at the foul line puts him at a disadvantage," he told his wife.

So Mr. F, wanting to help Sam make the best of a difficult position, casually strolled to third and gently guided Sam over a little to compensate for his being a lefty. In fact, he casually strolled over three or four times during that inning and gave Sam quite a few helpful hints. Now Mr. F was not one of those aggressive, sports-minded dads who had visions of a major leaguer. He just wanted his son to play his best and not feel frustrated. He wanted Sam to enjoy the game.

Mr. F, with the best of intentions, was doing what many parents do. He was trying to give his child a feeling of success and accomplishment by correcting the child, by telling him, "If you just do it this way instead of the way you're doing it now, you'll do a better job." This is clearly an approach that maximizes the importance of the end result—being a good third baseman.

What's wrong with that? Aren't there times when a little advice is in order? Yes, but advice and corrections need to be doled out in measured portions that decrease as the child exhibits more independence. When parents chronically offer help, help toward a good result, they are essentially robbing their children of the very feeling of success they are trying to achieve. They are robbing their children of feeling proud of what they can do independently, of a belief in themselves. Quite honestly, kids are less encouraged by our helpful hints than we would like to think. And, believe it or not, improvement comes naturally over time. What could Mr. F, or any other parent, have done instead?

He could have begun by translating many of those comments that correct to comments that encourage. He could have offered the kind of encouragement that is not solely results-oriented by turning his attention from a good job with a good result to a job well done whatever the result. He could have focused on the following four areas—

- effort and improvement
- problem-solving ability
- attitude
- intention

—so Sam would learn to see his small successes along the way.

✳ *Focus on Effort and Improvement*

Let's start by showing how one mother, Mrs. U, and her son, Jonathan, got so caught up in hoping for a good result that they failed to see the opportunity for encouragement that was right before their eyes.

Mrs. U was aware that Jonathan was not particularly pleased with his school performance. Neither was she, but she was fast learning that encouragement was the best motivator for Jonathan, and she was working hard to give it to him. On one afternoon that really stuck in her mind, she found Jonathan at the kitchen table with his books open, chewing on a pencil eraser and staring off into space. She was tempted to sit down next to him and make sure he started to get his work done, and, of course, Jonathan urged her on.

"Mom, I have a social studies test tomorrow. I just can't do it. Will you help me?"

"Of course," Mrs. U replied automatically.

She sat down beside him and started to plow in. After fifteen minutes she was as discouraged as he was about his getting a good grade on the test. Neither of them saw anything to be positive about.

What Mom and Jonathan were doing was concentrating very hard on the result, the grade on the test. Wasn't that the goal? No, not necessarily. Mrs. U and Jonathan needed to take a couple of steps back. Mrs. U could have changed her focus and helped Jonathan change his. She could have looked at the big picture.

Every goal requires completion of a series of steps. When parents or kids set their sights on the A on a test, for example, they lose track of the steps it takes to prepare for the test—the organization of work, the setting of priorities, and the skills of self-motivation and self-discipline. When you look at the components for reaching a goal, it's easy to see the importance of the steps along the way. The grade—whether an A or a D—will soon be forgotten. The skills involved in getting there will aid a child wherever she goes in life.

Mrs. U needed to begin to see the small successes along the way so Jonathan could feel encouraged even when the results were not what he had hoped for. His mom could not have known if Jonathan would get a good grade on the test the next day, but rather than wait for the test results and focus exclusively on a good grade, she could have commented on the effort he put forth in his studying. She could have pointed out the improvement in his willingness to tackle the work.

"I noticed you really improved in your ability to concentrate for a long time. We've been working here for over thirty minutes straight." [focus on effort and improvement]

"It looks like you are putting a lot of effort and thought into answering those questions at the end of the chapter." [focus on effort and improvement]

In this way, Jonathan could have been encouraged for the steps he was taking toward his goal—regardless of the final result.

There are a multitude of opportunities for you to comment on your child's effort and improvement. As you alter your focus, remember, it's important to be as specific as possible so your child can really experience a feeling of accomplishment and see for herself how she has improved.

Here are three additional examples of how you can focus on your child's effort and improvement:

> *"I can see a lot of improvement on the spelling paper in the way you make your letters."*

> *"You put a lot of effort into choosing colors that go together for that collage you made in art class."*

> *"You've really improved in your sewing. Now you're able to do an entire seam on your own."*

✳ *Focus on Problem-solving Ability*

In addition to focusing on effort and improvement, you can broaden your ability to build self-esteem by focusing on your child's problem-solving ability and ideas. A parent in one of our workshops volunteered the following story as she proudly related her broadened ability to encourage her child. It's a perfect example of what we mean.

It was the evening of February 13, and Judy was doing what millions of other children in America were doing—making herself a valentine box for school. She had wanted glitter to decorate her box, but her mom hadn't wanted to drive around looking for an open store. After a moment or two of last-ditch attempts to get glitter, Judy had secluded herself, busily cutting and pasting. After about an hour, she presented her mother with a wonderful valentine box that had as much sparkle as if she'd had the glitter she wanted. She had glued cold cereal onto her box, then painted it with some gold paint that was left over from her brother's Alaska Gold Rush project. What a "golden opportunity" for her mother to call attention to Judy's resourceful idea!

> *"What a great idea you had for giving your valentine box that glittery look. You sure are resourceful." [focus on problem-solving ability]*

Mom could have complimented the product, too, saying, "The box looks super." There's nothing wrong with acknowledging a good product, but by commenting on Judy's problem-solving ability, she also highlighted the value of being resourceful.

Here's another story of a child who clearly has been encouraged to problem-solve. Her mother, Mrs. R, felt she took it too far, but no one can deny that her daughter came up with a solution.

Emily, a child who would charm the pants off anyone, managed to keep her mom on her toes with her boundless energy. As Mrs. R laughingly says, "There is never a dull moment with Emily around." One afternoon Emily wanted some ice cream. They had none at home, but Mrs. R had put it on her grocery list and was planning to get some tomorrow. When she heard this news, Emily didn't complain; in fact, she didn't say another word about it. She just disappeared. Naturally, her mom thought she had forgotten about it. Instead, Emily went to her piggy bank, took out a dollar, and marched over to the neighbor's house. "Can I buy some ice cream from you? I have a dollar." The neighbor laughed, gave Emily ice cream, and refused the money. Emily was delighted. She still had the dollar, and the ice cream to boot.

Most parents will agree that Emily is a resourceful and determined child. She has true entrepreneurial spirit, the kind that so many times we adults unknowingly squelch. We may feel embarrassed by "nontraditional" behaviors, as Emily's mother did.

Mrs. R knew she would have to set some limits and tell Emily not to try to buy food from the neighbor anymore. But before she corrected Emily, she complimented her daughter on her problem-solving strategy. "I have to admit, that was very resourceful of you, Emily. You came up with a solution I never would have thought of." And she meant it.

As Emily's case shows, you can set limits on a child's behavior and at the same time encourage his creativity.

This brings up a very important point. There will be many times when correcting or limit-setting is called for. But when you can add to it some comments that build self-esteem, you accomplish two things: You don't let the negative outshine the positive; and you increase the likelihood that your child can hear you without becoming defensive and argumentative.

Whether you use these comments along with a comment that corrects your child or use them alone, you won't be able to ignore the smiles of pride on your child's face.

As you begin to notice your child's problem-solving skills, you can use the following phrases to encourage his ingenuity:

"What a clever idea."

"Good thinking."

"You sure solved that problem."

"I like that idea."

"I can't believe you thought to do that."

* Focus on Attitude

Another piece of the self-esteem puzzle is the ability to focus on a child's attitude. How many parents have watched their children maintain a positive attitude despite discouraging results and failed to comment on that attitude—noting instead how the children could improve their skills?

It's a hard lesson to learn, but it can make all the difference. Here's an example of how one mother was able to focus on attitude in order to help her daughter minimize the importance of mistakes and see the value of her hard work.

Vanessa was as ready as any little girl could be for her piano recital. She was decked out from her pretty shoes to the bow in her hair. Mom, Dad, and Grandma sat in the audience eagerly awaiting her two-and-a-half-minute piece. When it was Vanessa's turn, she sat down, placed her fingers on the keys, and started to play. As it turned out, she started her piece three times because she kept making the same mistake. Mom, an excellent pianist herself, could feel her stomach begin to knot up as she moved her own fingers in the air finishing the piece for Vanessa. At the end of her piece, three minutes later— probably forever to Vanessa—she got up from the bench, took her bow, and ran off the stage, ignoring the applause. After everyone had a turn, Mom and Dad greeted Vanessa's glum face with understanding smiles and said,

> *"You're really upset that you had to start over." [identify the feeling and nail down the specific event]*

They couldn't ignore their daughter's discouragement. Vanessa was well aware of her mess-ups. But what her parents also did was encourage Vanessa's "stick-to-it" attitude.

"I really admire the way you hung in there and finished your song, Vanessa. A stick-with-it style is really special." *[focus on attitude]*

Sure, Vanessa felt bad about the recital, but she had something she could put in her pocket and hold on to, so to speak. With the help of her parents, she could see herself as a kid with tenacity. By commenting on her persistent attitude, Vanessa's mom is showing her that the result is not the only measure of a job well done.

If you need to offer some helpful advice, that's okay. A lot of parents could not let such a situation go by without saying,

"Vanessa, if that would happen again, you might want to finish out the piece without starting over. No one in the audience would be the wiser."

This is a reasonable piece of advice that might be helpful to Vanessa in the future. But if you do offer advice, do it in a way that doesn't overshadow the present good attitude. If you want to make a suggestion, surround it with a comment that compliments your child's attitude.

If focusing on your child's attitude feels a little unnatural, don't get discouraged. Sometimes parents have a more difficult time complimenting attitudes than final results. Let's face it, it is much easier to notice something that is concrete, such as a good grade or a home run. To help you single out attitudes, here are five common ones that deserve notice:

"I love your go-get-'em *attitude."*

"You really have a positive mental *attitude."*

"I admire your willing-to-learn *attitude."*

"I like your pay-attention *attitude."*

"I'm glad you have an I'm-willing-to-change *attitude."*

* Focus on Intention

Another approach that you can use to bolster self-esteem is focusing on your child's intention. By intention we mean the thought, purpose, or reason behind your child's action. Every parent knows there are countless times when children—with the best of intentions—end up with results that are discouraging.

A classic example is when a child is helping Mom or Dad do the dishes and breaks one. Here's a story one dad told along those very lines.

Mr. G's son actually offered to help with the dinner dishes one evening. After a fast recovery from the initial shock, Dad gratefully accepted. Joel started filling the kitchen sink and somehow—on his way to the bathroom—got sidetracked in front of the TV. It's easy to guess what happened next. The sink overflowed. Joel was no dummy; the minute he saw what had happened, he started cleaning up the water. Dad took the opportunity to acknowledge his intention.

"I know you really wanted to help me." [focus on intention]

This dad also had a sense of humor and added,

"I'm going to hold on to that thought as I wade through the kitchen while you clean this up."

This was a perfect opportunity for a parent to acknowledge his child's intention. Doing so took the sting out of the bad end result and showed Joel something positive about what he'd done.

Intention is a great source of encouragement—especially when you're desperate. Separating out the intention from the final result may not be something you would easily remember to do. There is a good chance, in fact, that you would never think of it. Here is a clue that will help you: When the results are disastrous, you can focus on intention. Usually a child's motive is positive, and you may as well capitalize on that by acknowledging it.

* * *

Until now, most of our examples have shown how to use encouragement when kids are feeling down. But don't limit yourself. These forms of encouragement are just as effective and welcome when your child is feeling great and has done something wonderful.

When your child proudly presents a B paper, it should become very natural for you to say,

"You really put a lot of effort into that book report—good going." [focus on effort and improvement]

Or:

"I loved the way you figured out how get to soccer practice and still go to the party." [focus on problem-solving ability]

"You really had a go-get-'em attitude that served you well. Congratulations on winning the relay." [focus on attitude]

"I can see you really wanted to get something special for your sister's birthday, and by the look on her face you sure did." [focus on intention]

As you practice these encouragement techniques, you are accomplishing two things: First and foremost, you are increasing situations where you can encourage your child and maximize his self-esteem. Second, by modeling you are teaching your child to encourage herself for the small accomplishments that can be found in almost every activity. As you continue to point out positive steps that your child may not even see, you teach her to open her own eyes to her abilities, ideas, and attitudes.

The rewards will be evident as your child begins making statements like "I know you wanted to take me to lunch because you like spending time alone with me," "I really did a lot better this week at spelling than last week," or "Wasn't that a great idea I had?" You'll soon see that teaching your child to find something, however small, that he can value about his own behavior is a wonderful, enduring gift—whether the results are great or not so great, whether your child is feeling fabulous or forlorn. Seeing the steps along the way will make your child a winner.

POINTS TO REMEMBER

1. Offer limited portions of advice and correction to your child. Remember, improvement comes from encouragement, not criticism.

2. Good results can always be a source of pride, but you can multiply esteem-building comments when you focus on your child's small steps as well.

3. When there is not much happening in the way of praiseworthy behavior, focus on intention to build your child's self-esteem.

4. Use the following skills to point out small successes:

> * *Focus on effort and improvement.*
>
> * *Focus on problem-solving ability.*
>
> * *Focus on attitude.*
>
> * *Focus on intention.*

A Final Note

Throughout this book we have focused on how parents can approach their children in ways that decrease chaos and arguing and increase responsible behavior and self-esteem. We have focused on typical situations that fill every parent's day, and we have given you some practical tools that will enhance your relationship with your child. We have tried to stress throughout this book that the very same methods that create healthy, solid parent-child relationships give your child the skills he will need throughout his life. As you use these methods to improve your relationship with your child, you also improve his ability to

- adapt to routine
- negotiate and compromise
- problem-solve and initiate action
- see himself as a responsible person in control of his own future
- resolve conflict
- value himself as a capable person who can learn from his mistakes as well as his successes.

These skills are the seeds for your children's success as they face life's many challenges. Along with this invaluable training, we must remember one final ingredient. That ingredient is how you treat yourself. There is nothing quite so powerful in teaching self-respect as parents' modeling this in the way they treat themselves. There is nothing quite so powerful in teaching understanding and compassion as when parents demonstrate this—not only toward their children but toward themselves as well. Remember: Take some time to take care of yourself, just as you want your children to take good care of themselves when they go out on their own.